G000038138

AUTOBIOGRAPHY
Eddie O'Brien
PROPERTY ENTREPRENEUR
Liverpool

EDDIE OBRIEN
AUTOBIGRAPHY

PROPERTY ENTREPRENEUR

My mother shouted to my father, "Quick George, grab the children. The Germans are coming." My father ran outside into the street.
He shouted to my brothers, George, Allan and sister Rosemary, to get into the house quickly and go under the stairs where we all huddled together.
Soon, we could hear the first bombs dropping on the nearby Docks. We lived in Southey Street, Bootle, Liverpool. It was the May blitz of 1941, late in the afternoon. Merseyside was suffering one of the heaviest air raids of the Second World War.
It is hard to imagine 600 German bombers queuing up to drop 500 tons of bombs on our city. Liverpool and Bootle were the nerve centres of the Battle of the Atlantic and the base of the legendary Johnny Walker, feared German U-Boat killer, with 25 kills to his credit.
The Germans were desperate to destroy Walker's headquarters on the Bootle Docks, which were a few streets away. The Docks were full of armaments and war material from America and tons of food essential for our survival in this country.
The bombing had gone on for months. A German news bulletin described the onslaught on Bootle as the heaviest raid on any British port. My mother Rose, a big stout woman, held me in a vice like grip. I was 11 months old.
My father George crouched down with his arms around Rosemary and Allan who were both under 5 years of age. My eldest brother, George, was hanging on to his mother's legs, screaming in terror.
"Jesus, Mary and Joseph," my mother kept saying over and over again. The house was shaking as 'thousands pound' bombs dropped on the houses nearby.
They were coming down like hailstones. The noise of the explosions and anti-aircraft fire was deafening. The bombing was relentless.
German bombers were like gaggles of geese swooping down to cause death and destruction. It must have been terrifying for parents not knowing if their families would survive the onslaught.

After a few hours a huge explosion blew the top half of the house away. We were looking straight up at the sky! The stairs had saved us from certain death.

"Are you alright Rose?"

"Yes George. Thank God. Are the children O.K.?"

"Apart from being badly shaken they are fine."

I was too young to take it all in. We were all trapped by fallen joists and rubble and choking with the dust and thick smoke.

"Help will come soon Rose, I'm sure," said my father, trying to reassure my mother who was near to collapse. It was no good shouting for help. It was nearly midnight.

A voice shouted out, "Hello! Is anybody in there?"

"We're trapped under the stairs!" My mother and father shouted in unison.

The rescuers shouted to other men to come over to help us.

"They're trapped under the stairs lads,"

Wooden joists and rubble had fallen from the head of the stairs to the floor below saving us from the falling bricks and debris.

Allan was the first to be handed to the rescuers.

"God this one 'as just shit 'himself!" the first man said.

"So would you if you had bombs dropping on your head," replied his mate. They got us out quickly.

We stood in the street in a sad little group, bewildered and stunned by the night's events. Half of the houses on both sides of the street had been flattened and the dead and dying lay in the road. Arms and legs were strewn along the gutters. The Air-Raid Warden came over and told us to make a run for the air-raid shelter in Marsh Lane, which was at the end of our street. My father was sitting in the gutter trying to get his breath back. He was not in good health and had not worked for some time.

My mother staggered over to him. She was carrying me in her arms and only had one free hand to help Dad to his feet. He was pale - ashen-faced. Mam took hold of my brother George's hand. Allan and Rosemary were at my father's side. The bombing was as heavy as it could be. Incendiary bombs floated down slowly, gathering momentum before exploding on impact and causing huge fires everywhere.

The Germans were good at their national sport - 'World War'! Germany - a nation of sheep being led by a mad shepherd. How they loved to kill! These were not Nazis. They were Germans first and foremost.

There *were* no Nazis in The First World War when Germans killed 20 million people. Let's have it right!

Only a German mother would murder her own six children as Mrs Gourbils did all for Fatherland and the Fuhrer.

Our little family hurried along as fast as it could go.

We turned the corner into Marsh Lane. My father fell to his knees.

He was about 20 feet behind us. Little George spotted him and cried out.

" Mam! Dad's fell over!"

We quickly turned back and ran towards him.

"You go Rose and take the kids. I can't make it," he gasped.

He was lying in the gutter.

Mam prayed. "Mother of God, help us. Dear God, save us".

But wasn't it God who was putting us through this?

People were running everywhere in panic.

A man, passing, stopped. "Can I help you, love?'

"We are trying to get to the air-raid shelter in Marsh Lane but my husband's not well. Could you help him?"

The man was huge; he looked like a big Docker. He picked my father up and slung him over his shoulder like a fireman would and literally ran to the shelter.

We all followed behind.

Desperate families were pushing and shoving to get into the shelter.

It was packed! We made it just inside the door. My mother turned to thank the big man but he had gone. Tired, hungry dirty but still alive we settled in the corner by the door. Huddled next to us was the O'Connell family from Spencer Street.

"Thank God your family's safe Rose. Jesus, Mary and Joseph we are going through hell!" Mrs O'Connell said. "Why do they have to bomb our homes and children? Why can't the Germans just bomb the Docks? The only good German is a dead one."

We soon fell fast asleep huddled together but not for long. A bomb landed on the far end of the shelter. People were screaming and fighting to get out now. We were lucky to be right by the door. We scrambled out but others were jammed in the doorway. Some, who had escaped, went back to pull people clear who were trapped.

Whole families were slaughtered. People were running in all directions but they had nowhere to run.

German fighter-bombers were swooping down to machine-gunning families as they fled cutting them in half all for the Fatherland,.

What mentality must these animals have.

It was getting light now.

The Germans had finished their 8-hour shifts. They would now fly safely back across Southern Ireland because Ireland was neutral. Having said that, many Irishmen and women fought on the side of the British.

The local swimming baths was used as a temporary mortuary.

Mothers, fathers, brothers and sisters were being laid out side by side with tiny babies and the elderly.

Mass graves were dug at Anfield Cemetery for a 1,000 at a time.

"Let's go home George and see what's left." We trundled round to Southey Street. There were huge craters in the road. Half the street, on both sides, lay in ruins. All that we had left was what we standing up in we sat in despair in the gutter.

"The baby stinks Mam," Little George piped up, holding his nose.

"I know he hasn't had his bum washed since yesterday."

My father spotted a young woman pushing a pram on the far side of the road. "Look Rose, she might have a spare nappy. Go and ask her."

"Yoo Hoo!" Mam called. The girl stopped. My mother crossed the road and spoke to the girl.

"Do you have such a thing as a spare nappy? We've lost everything in the
bombing."

"*You have* lost everything!" Her face was swollen and one eye closed. There was blood down the front of her dress.

"*You've* lost everything!" She continued. "*You've* lost everything! I have lost my baby. Blown to bits. I found his head in the street and *you've* lost everything!"

She began to cry and was obviously traumatized. My mother moved closer to give her a hug. She looked down into the pram. It was empty. The girl spoke. "I'm sorry. Here, take the pram I don't need it anymore." She turned sharply and walked quickly away. There were no therapists or counsellors in those days. People had to get on with it.

And they did. There were no any nappies in the pram but there were a couple of sheets, which my mother tore up to make nappies for me.

The Salvation Army came round with tea and jam 'butties'. People were walking around in a daze. Some were digging through the rubble looking for their loved ones.

The Air-Raid Warden was asking people if they had any relations they could go to outside the bombing zone. My father, being Irish from County Cork, had none locally but my mother had a sister.

She lived in Aughton Green near Ormskirk, just outside Liverpool.

Her name was Mildred and was married to a wealthy Italian businessman. She was also a devout Catholic. When she wrote to anyone she would always enclose a novena or holy picture.

"That's good news George, They are going to lay on some transport as soon as they can. We have got to get away before the next German raid."   At about 9.a.m. a battered coal lorry turned up with no windscreen and the passenger side damaged. So we had to sit on the back.   Not that it bothered us we just wanted to get to safety.

I'm Tommy," said the driver, a typical Scouser with a heart of gold. They would give you their last halfpenny. He helped my father on, then George, Rosemary and Allan. My mother passed me up to the back of the cab with Dad then she got on herself. We sat against the back of the cab with our parents on either side, kids in the middle.

I was soon fast asleep. Tommy tied the pram to the back end of the lorry over the wheels.

The neighbours that were left waved us 'goodbye'.

Tommy drove down Southey Street then turned into Marsh Lane and along Stanley Road, up Linacre Lane and onto Ormskirk.

" 'Mildred will be glad to see us George. We can have a bath and a decent meal. The kids must be starving".

The journey took a bout 40 minutes. We stopped outside a huge detached house. We disembarked and walked up the sweeping driveway. We looked like refugees. In a way we were. Mother rang the bell. There was no answer.

She waited and rang again. Still there was no response.

"She must be at Mass George. I forgot it's Sunday morning."

Mam rang a third time. She stepped back and looked up at the upstairs window.

Auntie Mildred was peeping out from behind the curtain. When she saw my mother looking up, Auntie quickly put the curtain back.

My mother turned to my father and said, "There's 'no room at the Inn' George." We walked back down the drive. Tommy had just untied the pram and was wheeling it towards us.

Dad said, "There's no answer Tommy. We will have to go back into the bombing"

My mother asked Tommy to take us to, "The Alexander", a pub in Marsh lane, which was run by her sister Nellie.

She also had another sister who lived in the Bedford Road but she thought we would be safer at the pub as we would be able to take

refuge in the cellar when the bombing started again. We clambered aboard the lorry once again and set off for "The Alexander".
Back into the bombing we went.
"The Alexander" was known locally as "The Stadium" as there were so many fights there! Auntie Nellie ran the pub with her husband Tommy Larkin. They had three sons, Bob, Chris and Jimmy and four daughters, Pat, Rita, Joan and Marie. We were made very welcome.
We all had a hot bath and a big plate of scouse. Just after tea, the air-raid warning kicked off. Mam and Dad were just listening to the wireless.
"Come on everybody, down to the cellar." Auntie Nellie shouted.
We heard the drone of the aircraft engines as they passed overhead, then they would unleash their cargo of death and destruction. This went on hour after hour. Luckily for us, we got through this particular night unscathed. There had been a two-day lull in the bombing so, after breakfast the next morning,
My father said, "Come on Rose, let's take the kids down to the North Park. We'll take them out for a walk; they've not been out for weeks. It will also give Nellie a break they will be out from under their feet."
It was noon before we got on our way and we walked down to the North Park on Stanley Road.
"How anyone survived the devastation George, I will never know."
My mother remarked as they looked at house that been flattened in the raids. We spent a couple of hours in the park. It was a bright sunny day and a number of families were having a break from the bombing, which they knew was only temporary.
Mam had an idea. "I know George, let's go and see Shaddy, see if she's alright."
Shaddy was an old friend of my mother's. She lived on her own in a little terraced house by Saint James' church.
We were invited in and Shaddy made a pot of tea and gave us some home- made scones. "I will put the light on Rose it is a bit dull"
She lit a taper and turned on the gas and the globe popped as it ignited. The talk was about the 'Blitz', who had been killed, who had survived and who was missing, they had a good chat for an hour or so.
"I heard your street was bombed Rose you were very fortunate to escape. Thanks be to God that you and your family survived Rose and may the good Lord look after you and preserve you." Shaddy said blessing herself.
"We are staying with our Nellie at the pub Shaddy."
"You look tired George. I suppose it's getting to all of us isn't it?"

"We had better be getting back to the pub Shaddy,"
"It will be tea-time shortly. It's been lovely seeing you."
"And you Rose,"
"I was worried about you." "Goodbye and God bless Shaddy."
We set off back to the pub.

We had only gone a couple of streets when the air-raid warning sounded. We started to hurry. George and Rose were hanging on to each side of the pram. People were running for their lives. Father and Allan were falling behind.

The Docks were being pounded and we were next. Huge barrage balloons in the sky were waiting for the German bombers to crash into them but few did.

We waited on the corner by "The Salisbury" pub for Dad and Allan to catch up. We crossed over to Marsh Lane.

"Not too far to go now George," my mother said with great relief."
Bombs were exploding all round us now. Whole families were being blown to bits. Thick dust and smoke everywhere was choking us.

We were just a few yards from the pub door when my mother tripped over a loose leg and lost her grip of the pram. Father let go of Allan's hand to grab the pram and help Mam to her feet. You could hardly see a hand in front of you.

My father lifted me out of the pram and we were taken down into the cellar. My mother's knees were bleeding. The pub shook from a near miss.

"Where's Allan? Where's Allan?" my mother screamed.

He was nowhere to be seen. "Quick George, Allan's not with us, he's not made it!"

My mother was screaming. "Let me out, let me out, my son's out there."
People restrained her and Auntie Nellie came over to comfort her.

"There is no way you can go out there now Rose," she said.

The pub shook again from a nearby blast.

Little Allan, only 3 years old, was running around in the bombing. It continued all night and poor mother cried inconsolably. At 4.a.m.the raid ceased

My parents searched all day for Allan without a sign of him. They called at Marsh Lane Police Station but the police said that there were hundreds of people missing but they took details and suggested that Mam and Dad tried the mortuary.

They called in at St. James' church and Mam knelt down in front of the statue of St. Anthony, the patron saint of lost causes, who was her favourite saint.   "Please St. Anthony you've found my purse for me in the past, please find my son."

My father said the Rosary and then they made the Stations of the Cross. "We had better have another look around Rose before the bombing starts again."

My father started to cry. "It's all my fault Rose. I should have kept hold of his hand."

"It's not your fault George you did your best."

They returned to the pub just before tea. They were worn out and no sign of little Allan. We had just finished our meal when the siren went again. The Germans were coming so it was the cellar once more.

We settled in the corner but my parents could not sleep.

My mother was sobbing quietly. My father had his arms around her trying to console and reassure her. She looked up at him and said,.

"I know what that young mother felt like now George, the one who gave us the pram. How can Allan survive out there in this carnage he is only three years old. "Don't think like that Rose try and get some sleep"

I think at the time that they both thought that Allan was dead but neither of them would admit it to each other .

It was a wonder that there was anything left to bomb.

Mam and Dad set out again the next morning and spent all day asking people if they had seen a little boy on his own. People were very helpful but they were looking for their own relatives and friends. There was no photograph of Allan because our house had been bombed. There were hundreds of children missing or killed.

Auntie Nellie could see by the look on my parent's faces that they had drawn another blank when they came back in the afternoon. So it was the same procedure, tea, cellar, bombing.

Rosemary and George were crying wanting to know when their little brother was coming back. Mam and Dad set out again the next day at about 8 a.m.

At 12 noon there was a loud continous knock on the door.

"Alright! Keep your hair on," Auntie Nellie shouted.

"I'm coming." The knocking continued until the door was opened. An attractive girl was standing there in her a young teenager. In her arms was little Allan.

He immediately launched himself into Auntie Nellie's arms, hugging her. His arms tightened around her neck.

Nellie was overjoyed and asked the young girl into the pub.

"Please come through to the back and have a seat."

The young lady sat at the kitchen table.

Auntie Nellie put little Allan down then called George and Rosemary. They rushed in to hug and kiss him, all of them ending up on the floor hugging each other. Auntie Nellie turned to the young woman.

"Tell us everything, how when and where did you find him?"

"It was 3 nights ago. I was running back home down Stanley Road facing North Park. He was near the bottom of the lane screaming in terror. It was total panic. People were dashing everywhere. The only thing I could do was to take him home. I had to wait until the bombing was over. The next morning I took him to the police station at Marsh Lane. They said that there were hundreds of missing and homeless children. The next couple of days I must have asked dozens of people if they knew him. Then this morning, I came down the bottom of the lane and a man said that there was a little boy missing from the pub. So here I am."

" Auntie Nellie's eyes filled with tears. She took hold of the girl, hugged her and said, "His parents are out looking for him. They have been out of their minds with worry.

I don't know what time they will be back. They shouldn't be long. Would you like a cup of tea?"

The girl, looking tired and weary, declined the offer.

"No thanks, I have to go. My mother has been hurt in the bombing and she has lost a leg. She is on 'urgent note' at Stanley Road Hospital. I have to go and see her."

" Leave your name and address his parents will want to thank you.

Mam and Dad had been searching all morning. They had walked miles. They called in at St. James' church again. After praying they both sat at the back of the church.

"It's been 3 days now George. We have to face it. We will have to go to the mortuary like the policeman said."

"No, Rose, let's give it another day. There are rows of children in the mortuary with arms and legs missing. you can't take that."

"We will go back to the pub George, you look all in. We will have a few hours rest and try again".

They had just got through the front door of the pub when George and Rosemary came running out shouting ." He`s back Mam Allans back "

With that Allan came running out my Mam swept him up in her arms squashing the life out of him. Dad was beside himself. He had his arms around both of them. Mother was crying with joy.

After everyone had calmed down . Auntie Nellie explained to my parents how the young girl Kathy Murphy had turned up with Allan this

morning. "I hope it wasn't long before she found him.
He must have been terrified.
We will have to go and thank her as soon as possible".
Everyone was so happy. Allan was like his mother's shadow. He would follow her and sit on her knee all the time. No way was he losing sight of her again.

The next morning we all went round to Kathy Murphy's on Stanley Road to thank her for saving little Allan's life. Dad was knocking on the door when a next-door neighbour came out and said that there was nobody at home.

My mother said, "We come to see Kathleen Murphy".

The neighbour said, "You're too late. Kathleen and her sister had been to visit their mother. When they arrived at the hospital they were told their mother had died. On the way home they were killed in the bombing and blown to bits there will be no funeral she was just sixteen. "

The bombing continued. The Germans thirst for blood unquenchable. Ask any Jew.

A little while later the authorities decided to move us out of the bombing zone to a new council estate at 'Huyton- with-Roby' on the outskirts of Liverpool towards St Helens'. Coaches and buses were laid on

All the community helped each other. Catholics and Protestants all helped each other.

You can't help what religion you are born into. If you are born a Catholic you are a Catholic. If you are born a Protestant you are a Protestant. Nobody plans it so what does it matter what religion you are, it is your own private business. We were allocated 135 Pennard Avenue Huyton.

On the left at 133 were Mr and Mrs Bullock and their three sons David, Brian and Donald.

On the other side at 137 were Mr and Mrs Hanagh; their grandson in the future would become world champion boxer John Conteh.

My parents had the front bedroom. George and Allan were in the back bedroom and Rosemary in the box room. We had a bathroom, front and rear garden.

Across the road there was a German prisoner of war camp behind a high barbed wire fence. Most of our neighbours were from Bootle. It was like another world away from the bombing. The months rolled by and great joy was bestowed upon our family.

A little bundle arrived, who we christened Joseph, a beautiful baby boy. I now had a younger brother. He brought great happiness to my parents

After all they had been through.

All the neighbours made a great fuss of Joseph, as he was the first baby born in the street. As little Joseph was being carried around Allan would be hanging on to mother's skirt. If a plane flew over he would run under the table and hide shouting, "Mam, Mam they are throwing bombs at me again". He was obviously affected by the trauma he had suffered. Friends and neighbours would knit baby clothes for Joseph and when mother would wheel him down the street, people would stop her wanting to look and admire him.

She was never happier. A few months later little Joseph was taken ill. "I think we had better get the Doctor George. He does not look well at all".

My father went for the doctor and he came within half an hour.

Little Joseph had been brought down stairs. He was lying in the wardrobe drawer, which was being used as a cot. The doctor examined little Joseph. "He has a temperature Mrs. O'Brien. Keep him warm. Give him some sugar in warm water and I will call again in the morning".

After the doctor left my father said, "Rose he does not seem to know what is wrong he seemed a bit vague didn't he?"

My father's face was full of anguish as he put a protective arm around mother's weary shoulders.

"You bank the fire up George and I'll stay up all night."

She tucked a blanket around her precious infant.

"We will keep Joseph down here in the warmth".

My father built up the fire with slack and coal kissed my mother and went upstairs. Mam stayed in the armchair all night with little Joseph at her feet.

My father came down stairs at 7 am and shook my mother.

"Rose wake up the baby's hardly breathing".

My mother jumped up quickly and picked Joseph up.

"Hurry George get the doctor as fast as you can!"

The doctor came about 20 minutes later. He lifted little Joseph onto the table and put the stethoscope to his chest.

"Mother of God save him, Sacred Heart of Jesus, help us in our hour of need. St Anthony pray for us". My mother kept repeating the prayers over and over.

The doctor covered little Joseph's head. He turned to my mother and said, "I'm afraid he's dead, I think it was meningitis".

"No, no he can't be dead he's only 10 weeks old. God almighty"!

My mother cried out. Mother picked up little Joseph and held him to her chest. My mother's cries woke up the other children.

We all came down stairs. Mother was sitting in the armchair holding little Joseph.

"What's the matter Mam?" George junior asked.

"I'm afraid little Joseph's dead". She was sobbing uncontrollably.

Everybody started to cry as we watched our mother in her grief.

The undertaker Mr Dundon was a big tall man all dressed in black with a bowler hat. He lived in the street behind us Shepton Road He placed little Joseph`s little white coffin on the table.

Friends and neighbours came in to comfort my parents and pay their respects.

The priest came around that evening full of 'comfort'!

"Has the baby been baptized, if he has not he will not go to the Kingdom of Heaven?"

My father confirmed that he had been baptized.

Our next door neighbour Mrs Bullock, a Protestant, asked the other neighbour Ginny Privelage, a Catholic, why a baby can't go to the Kingdom of Heaven if it has not been baptized.

Ginny Privelage said all Catholic babies are born with original sin on their souls and they are not allowed into the Kingdom of Heaven until it is Baptized.

Mrs Bullock asked how a newborn baby could be guilty of sin and not allowed into the Kingdom of Heaven. It wouldn't be the baby's fault so why punish it? Mrs Bullock waited for the answer.

Ginny shook her shoulders and said, "I don't know why.

The funeral took place two days later. Mr Dundon carried the little white coffin out to the hearse, which was drawn by two black horses. My parents followed behind.

My mother could hardly stand. Some of the German prisoners across the road stood to attention with bare heads. He was buried at Yew Tree Cemetery. His little white coffin was passed down into the grave. It looked like a shoebox dwarfed by the big hole. After every funeral people say life goes on but what a life. What is it all about? There was an air of sadness in the house and numbness as though life had stopped.

The following weeks my parents just sat around the house not knowing what to say or do. My mother could not stop crying. Joseph's death had devastated them and with all the bombing and Allan going missing it all had taken its toll.

Just three months after Joseph's funeral my father was taken ill.

"I'll think I'll stay in bed this morning Rose I don't feel too good".

"I'll bring you some tea and toast up George".

She went back up about an hour later. He had drunk the tea but left the toast. He was fast asleep.

She turned and looked back as she got the bedroom door.

My father's a big man; tall, dark curly hair, a handsome man; now he looked so fragile.

He looked as though he was sinking into the mattress.

On the third day he was in great pain. "No doctor please Rose".

Mother could not bear to see his suffering and ignored his plea.

My mother ran and got the doctor, he gave my father morphine for the pain and he fell into a deep sleep.

Downstairs the doctor told George Jnr, Rosemary, Allan and myself to go out of the room.

"Your husband is gravely ill Mrs O'Brien, and I'm afraid it is Cancer. I will call everyday".

My mother collapsed to the floor, with a struggle he managed to get her into the armchair. "Here take two Aspirin".

He sent George Jnr to get a neighbour it was my mother's closest friend Ginny Privalege. The doctor left and the four of us went in.

All of us at the same time tried to climb on the armchair and hug her as she was crying .

"What's the matter Mam, are you crying about little Joseph dying?" Rosemary asked.

"No children, your daddy's not well and I got a little upset, don't worry I will be all right".

Ginny Privelage said, "What next Rose, this is purgatory".

The doctor came the next morning as promised and gave my father some morphine for the pain. My father had been ripping the sheets during the night. In the early evening we all went in to see him.

He had just woken up. "All the children are here to see you George". Mam said, trying to sound cheerful. We sat around the bed; he gave us a lovely smile but could hardly talk. We stayed for about twenty minutes then my mother said he was getting tired so we all went downstairs to listen to the wireless.

He deteriorated badly over the next five days and he was in agony.

My mother was sitting on the side of the bed it was about midnight, she could see him grimacing with pain. "George listen to me. Can you hear me?" He gave a slight nod of his head.

"George don't fight on, I know you are clinging on to stay with us. Let go the pain is too much. You go we will all meet again in heaven. Just let go".

She squeezed his hand for the last time.

When she went in to see him again at 5 am he had died in his sleep.

His coffin was put on trestles in the front room, the lid standing up against the wall by the fireplace. The same people came and paid their respects to my father, just as they had to baby Joseph.

My aunts paid for my father's funeral and got their own undertakers, Tiernans of Old Swan. How much more could my mother take?

On the day of the funeral, the neighbours came to give their support. The German prisoners all lined up again. We got in the front of the car with our mother.

They opened Joseph's grave and laid my father on top of him.

My mother cried all the way there; she was near to collapse at the graveside.

That night when everyone had gone home, my mother said,

"Let's bring the two big mattresses down and we will sleep on the floor and keep the fire going, we will all be together. Get some coal George, fill the bucket and bank the fire up with slack".

We all ended up on one mattress, huddled together and cried ourselves to sleep.

A couple of Sundays after the funeral, Mr Dundon the undertaker, a devout catholic who had buried Joseph, was coming home from mass at St Columbus church. He had to pass our house on the way home he gave my mother a telling off for not burying my father he left her in tears.

There are a lot of churchgoers about, but not many Christians.

We kept to the routine of sleeping on the front room floor.

A few weeks later we were all fast asleep, it was in the early hours when suddenly there was an almighty crash. The front door was kicked in.

We all jumped up. Through the open door staggered two big black Moroccan soldiers. They were drunk and could hardly stand.

"Where is Lucy, we want Lucy". They were yelling.

Lucy was the local bike

My mother pushed us into the corner and stood in front of us.

"You have got the wrong house, Lucy lives on the next block. Go further down the road". They staggered out holding each other up.

"God almighty help us".

What else could this loving merciful God put my poor mother through.

A few years later, getting towards the end of the war times were hard for everyone. My mother was bringing four children up on a widow's pension of a pittance. Food was rationed; she used to sell some of our ration book coupons to a Mr. Tinnot so he could get extra bacon, eggs and butter things that we could not afford. He used to pass the plate around in church that was before they caught him stealing the money. Every house had a bowl of beef dripping from which we made dripping butties; this sustained us during the day. We would have Scouse most days or on a bad day, blind Scouse `no meat`.

Some of the neighbours set off to Prescot coke works, about five miles away. They would take an old pram and fill it full of coke then walk back. George would take Joseph's pram and take me with him it was like a little wagon train of prams.

Any bits of spare clothing or old shoes people would throw over to the Germans in spite of what they had done.

The Germans made us clowns made up of two pieces of wood and elastic. Press the bottom of the wood and the clown would do a somersault.

One day my mother was looking out of the window at a German prisoner. He was holding his mouth and leaning on his spade. Obviously he was suffering with toothache. My mother went over and passed a bottle of toothache tincture through the barbed wire. She tried to explain that it was so strong that you had just to dab a bit on the tooth and it would kill the pain. It was powerful stuff but to no avail.

The German drank the whole lot and ended up on the floor in agony. The other Germans roared with laughter.

Also in the camp was a big blond German goalkeeper he could pick the case ball up with one hand half the length of the field. He was later to play for Manchester City; his name was Bert Trautman.

The prisoners would play the local pub The Bluebell it would end after ten minutes in a bloodbath. The war had just ended it was 1945.

The Germans demolished their camp and went home. This left a big space between our houses and the houses across the road, which we called `the olla`.

The houses, which were behind the camp, had been occupied by British and Commonwealth troops. We could now see up the Layford road opposite now. Everyone was delighted that the war was over and their loved ones would be coming home.

We were having dinner, which was a bowl of `pobs`, hot milk and bread. When my mother told us that our big brother was coming home. What a shock! We did not know we had a big brother; he was called Michael. He was my father's son from his first marriage. Father had been a widower when he married our mother but we were unaware of this fact at the time so we naturally assumed that Michael was my mother's son. We were not made aware of the facts until some years later.

I suppose Mam had her reasons for this. Apparently, when Michael was fifteen he joined the Irish Guards at the start of the war in 1939. He told them he was 16, the legal age to join up. His regiment was sent over to France. His mate John Murphy did the same thing. They found out that both of them were under age so they kept them both at the barracks. They were very lucky, for the Irish Guards regiment was wiped out a soon as they landed in France.

They were included in the next batch and shipped off to France. They were soon in the action, attacking a German machine gun post.

They were being cut down like a scythe cutting through grass.

All young lads, Michael and John stuck together, as they had been mates for years. As night fell the fighting stopped and they took cover in a trench with another lad called O'Neil. They had enlisted at the same time. John got his cigarettes out and handed them around.

" God it's my birthday today, Michael."

"Happy birthday John" Michael and O'Neil said simultaneously

They all laughed, John gave Michael then O'Neil a light, went to light his own and was shot through the head by a German sniper. The fatal third light!

A few days later they were over run and Michael was taken prisoner. He never saw O'Neil again. They were herded into lorries to be transported into a Prisoner of War camp. He was in the rear lorry in a convoy of six going through the French countryside. On the edge of a wood the convoy was stopped. The road was blocked by fallen trees. Most of the Germans went to help clear the road just leaving a couple of guards looking after the prisoners.

The guard at the rear was quickly overpowered and the lads in the last lorry made a run for it Michael included. They dispersed into the wood as fast as their legs would carry them, bullets whistling all around them. Michael kept on running until it was dark. He fell asleep exhausted in what he thought was a field.

Early next morning he was being prodded by a boot " wake up Tommy, wake up."

There was a man standing over him with a shotgun,.

"Come quickly to my farmhouse you can hide and I will give you some breakfast" he said in a French accent; "You are most welcome".

Michael followed him into the house, through into the kitchen.

"Sit there my friend at the table, I will get my wife to cook something for you.

" His wife came in, a big fat women, arse like a flock bed. She smiled at Michael and started to cook him ham and eggs.

The smell drifting over was wonderful, as he was famished.

The husband said something in French to his wife and then he left the room. She came over and handed him a cup of coffee. A few minutes later she came over and placed a plate of ham and eggs on the table.

"You are such a young boy, fighting in this terrible war, they should not allow it."

Michael tucked into his ham and eggs.

"Another coffee?"

"Yes please you are very kind".

What a lovely couple Michael thought. He had just put his knife and fork down when the door opened and in walked four German soldiers with the French Judas behind them.

Michael stood up but he was smashed in the face with a rifle butt. The Germans gave him a good kicking.

He ended up in Stalag 3 for the duration of the war.

This couple like most of the French were collaborators or cowards.

The French resistance handed over more of our R.A.F airmen than they saved. They even betrayed their own resistance leader to SS commander Clause Barbie, the Butcher of Lyons. he was tortured and executed   Beside that, we had to bomb the French Navy to stop them handing their ships over to the Germans, as the French Navy was too frightened to leave port to fight for their own country.   They then fought for the Germans bombing Gibraltar

The French tank had one forward gear and five reverse .

President De Gaulle French hero fled to England enough said!

The Germans guillotined 16,000 of their own countrymen for opposing Hitler even verbally

There was small resistance group called White Rose mainly young students .

They captured a young couple about to be married they had been printing anti Nazi leaflets After a brief trial they were sentenced to death both 18 years old

They cut her head of first it landed in the basket

 The Germans then placed him in the guillotine he was looking down at his beloved girlfriend head they let blade go it sliced his head clean off ,it landed next to hers the Germans cheered ,slaughtered all for the Fatherland.

There were no German war heroes if you leave your own country and slaughter innocent men women and children that is what the Germans enjoyed doing you were a murderer, not a hero.

There were big street parties organized for V.E. day, everybody joined their tables together the full length of the street. All the mother's made cakes and jellies and anything that was available. The kids were over the moon. Soon after, Michael came home, my mother was so happy as she had not seen him for six years. He was tall, very thin, his uniform hanging on him. She was crying with joy as they hugged each other. I had never seen her look so happy. Michael was like the Pied Piper. Everywhere he went my brothers and sister followed him.

I remember him taking me to Mrs Jones' house at 109 Pennard Avenue. In the front room they had huge wooden barrels of beer for the grown up's party. Michael only stayed with us for another year or so and then he *emigrated to Tasmania then Australia and finally settled in New* Zealand. We then lost touch completely.

Next door but one, at 131 lived a Welsh man they called 'Taffy', a big, fat Welsh bastard, he had been the camp cook for the German prisoners. One evening I had reason to visit this unsavoury person. It was teatime when I got to his front door, which open about 12 inches.

As I approached, I heard a woman crying then screaming. I looked in, he was beating his wife Rita, her eye was cut and there was blood running down her cheek.

He kept punching her I was frozen to the spot. He had her up against the wall; he punched her in the nose, her nose split open. Blood was running down her chin onto her chest, she slid down the wall and then he kicked her in the stomach.

She lay there unconscious; he turned and spotted me at the door.

He screamed at me, "What the fuck do you want?"

"Could I have my Dandy back please?" I stammered.

" Fuck off you little twat!"

He came towards me, I legged it as fast as I could.

That's the last time I'll lend him my comics! I ran home and told my Mam.

She went to see him. He grabbed her around the throat but she managed to break free and run. He chased her, grabbing the back of her cardigan. She was a few feet from the safety of our front door. She managed to slip out of her cardigan and get through the front door and slammed it shut. She sat on the stairs gasping for breath.

We played all the usual games, Elallio, Marbles, Hopscotch, Ducks and

Drakes. Some of the lads would make winter warmers by putting holes in a tin can, attached it to a wire, put pieces of paper and wood and light it and swing it around over our heads, keeping it going for hours.

When we found a lorry tyre one of the smaller boys would get in the middle and we would roll him down the hill on Woolfall Heath.

Most nights we would play football on the `olla` where the camp was. We would put our coats down, any other boy who wanted to join in would go `pudding and beef. Billy Roberts was the only one with a case ball, if he was fouled a few times or a goal disallowed he would sulk and take his ball home, ending the match. During these matches one of the mothers would come out and shout.

"Dick Barton's on", we would all dash in and listen to the wireless. Other programmes I liked were, `Paul Temple` and `Valentine Dahl - the Man in Black`.

One day, my mate next door, Brian Bullock, suggested we go pea picking` on the farms in Knowsley and Kirkby. We set out at six am. His brother David and our Allen and George all decided to come with us. We packed our jam butties and bottles of water in a haversack, and then we walked down Knowsley Lane, past Lord Derby's estate.

We called at a couple of farms, but there were dozen of people waiting to be taken on. A farm would only pick adults and mainly men.

We tried again the next couple of days without success, so in the end we gave it up as bad job.

I went to St Columbus school it was a mixture of huts and a big country house called the White House. The huts were heated with a coke stove in the centre of the room. There were about forty pupils in each class.

Every Monday our teacher Mr Morrison, would call out the register then take the dinner money from those who were staying for school meals, then he would say,

"Who's on free meals?" I would put my hand up, the only one in the class. My mother was only getting a widow's pension, which was a pittance so I was entitled to free dinners. Was he aware how he humiliated me every Monday morning. Any adult, let alone a teacher should have known. I don't know why he did it.

Some of the kids would snigger and make snide remarks.

On another day, the doctor and the nit nurse came to examine the class. The doctor would look at you first and then pass you on to the nit nurse. I felt uncomfortable, as the lads had to strip to the waist I knew my vest was full of holes, I asked the teacher if I could go to the toilets.

This was so I could take my vest off and throw it in the bin, he refused.

I stood in front of the Doctor. "Take your shirt and vest off of son"
I tried to get my vest over my head but got it all tangled. The doctor said,
"Never mind son I will put the stethoscope through one of the holes".
The other kids were in hysterics; I was called `Holy Eddie` for months
afterwards.

We were really struggling now my mother was having dizzy spells and
had high blood pressure with all the worry. There were no free
handouts or benefits from anywhere in those days but the Priest would
call around to collect money off her for church needs.

You would think that a widow with four children would get some help
from the church, even a loaf now and again. We were getting desperate,
cardboard in our shoes, no arse in our pants.

There were no shops nearby, so my mother decided to sell something
from the house. Ginny Privalege sold the Liverpool Echo from number
127. Mrs Savage sold toffee apples from number 111. In the next road,
Mrs Kirkwood sold everything. It was like a little general shop.

Ever resourceful, Mam decided to take advantage of the situation
herself. She resolved to start a small business, at the house hoping that
it would give us a extra few pounds a week. My mother opted for
lemonade, "Edmondson Full Swing" lemonade.

They had a big advertisement on Commutation Road in Liverpool, of a
girl on a swing all in lights, with `Edmondson Full Swing Lemonade
underneath.

It was against council regulations but others were breaking the rules by
selling goods from their own house. She had to go and see the local
moneylender for her starting capital of £20.

Mrs Grant a pillar of the Church, being a devout Catholic he only charged
the poor of the Parish 15% interest and took my mothers widowed
pension book as security.

A couple of days after the pop wagon rolled up, old Charlie, the driver
who came from Birkenhead, he brought the 10 crates into the hall and
suggested we take the bottles out of the crates to save paying the three
shillings deposit on the crates.

Word soon got around the estate and we sold out the first week. There
was only a penny profit per bottle but was a great help at the time, my
mother would order a few extra crates each week.

After a couple of weeks he took us all to the wholesalers, Gilmans in
Islington in Liverpool, to try other lines such as, Babies' dummies,
"Cherry Blossom" boot polish, Double EE powders, razor blades and back
and front studs. As a treat we went to T J Hughes on London Road for

our dinner of sausage and chips. We were living it up now!

I thought it would help if I took a shoe box around the houses with some small lines e.g. razor blades, boot polish, babies dummies and shoe laces. I started in Layford Road.

I knocked on the door of the first house, "Do you want to buy any Blue Gillette, Red Gillette, Green Gillette razor blades or babies' dummies?"

" Piss off!" the man shouted and shut the door in my face. Not a good start .

At the next house I sold a baby dummy and two Double EE powders and nothing at the third.

The fourth house I knocked on the door a Policeman answered the door in his uniform.

"Do you want to buy any Red Gillette, Blue Gillette, Green Gillette razors?"

He leaned forward and snatched the shoe box off me,

"Where did you get these from, have you stolen them?" He barked, holding onto my shirt collar.

" No I am selling them for my Mother as we have no father."

An older man appeared at the door, " Give the kid the bloody box back." He took the box off the policeman and gave it back to me.

I did all Layford Road about 20 houses and took £1=7=6d. My mother was very pleased and so was I. We charged 2d deposit on each bottle the only problem was that people would come back after midnight with their empty bottles in order to get their dads' fare for work.

On a Wednesday, a Miss Scattergood would come around to collect the rent for the Council. We could not open the door because of the goods on sale, so we gave our rent to Ginny Privalege to pay it for us.

We were worried in case anyone brought empty bottles back to the house while Miss Scattergood was near.

So George, Allan, Rosemary and myself would stand on each corner of the avenue with some change in case anyone brought empties back.

The money from the shop was not a fortune but it meant that we did not have to sell our ration food coupons to Mr Tinnet from the Church.

It was approaching Easter Weekend so my mother ordered fifty crates of lemonade.

Old Charlie came with his "Full Swing" lemonade wagon on Friday we all got stuck in and emptied the fifty crates out and laid the bottles on their side in the hall and up the stairs. Charlie put the empties back on the wagon and sat down in the kitchen for a cup of tea he was all in.

The next thing there was a knock on the front door, my mother opened the door, two men stood there.

" We are from the council, it is against Council Regulation to use a Council House as a shop, you could face eviction, now get all this stuff out of here at once you will be reported."

We had to put the bottles back into the grates and put it back on the wagon.

" Somebody has snitched on you the bastards won`t let you live".

Charlie said how sorry he was, gave my mother the money back and left. We were just getting on our feet when that happened.

Mother was nearly in tears, " By the time we pay Mrs Grant back plus the interest and there are still empty bottles to refund deposits. We will be back to square one".

We found out later on that it was Mrs Francis Haskayne next but one at 139 who had informed the council, another churchgoer. As I say a again lot of churchgoers but not many Christians. George and Allan were Alter Boys, when Father Lawler came around collecting he said he wanted me to come to evening classes to learn Latin and join my brothers on the alter. I found it very difficult to be honest I was hopeless, you don't understand what you are saying then you have to know when to ring the bell. A month later George informed me the 3 of us were to serve the 7 a.m. next Sunday. I was petrified Allan said don't worry he would ring the bell. My Mam was delighted that her 3 sons were serving Mass together and said she attend and thank Jesus on this great occasion.

I pleaded with her not to go as I would be to nervous with her present she agreed and said she would go another time thank God.

There were only a couple of dozen people in the congregation. It was getting near Holy Communion time George had carried the Missal to the right hand side of the Alter for the priest to read I was kneeling very close to his left side George and Allan to his right. As I looked to my right I spotted a two shilling piece just to the right of the priest foot I leant across to pick it up he stepped back and went head over heals down the alter steps and ended up against the alter rails.

Not a happy man, I was never asked again serve again and he took the two-shilling piece of me as well.

I was now aged thirteen. I played football all the hours I could. My mate Jimmy Morgan heard of a team in the Liverpool Boys Association League. The manager was a Mr Mac from 6 Lampeter rd Anfield and the trainer was called George The team was called Stardale but there were not many stars in it and we lost a lot more than we won.

I was also very interested in Boxing. In 1953 our British Heavyweight

Champion, Don Cockell, was fighting Rocky Marciano for the heavyweight championship of the world in the USA.

It was to be broadcast on the wireless at 3 am.

George, Allen and myself decided to stay up to listen.

We played cards and messed about until 3 am. George switched the wireless on. Not a cough, not a sound came through. George banged and shook the wireless but to no avail.

We read in the paper the next day that Cockell got K.O`d in the ninth round after putting up a valiant effort.

Like most young boys my dream was to be a professional footballer, but there were thousands of boys with the same dream few were chosen.

One or two of the local lads went for trials at Everton and Liverpool and they found out it didn't matter how good you were there was a lot of favouritism at both clubs if your dad or uncle knew someone at the club you would get picked before more gifted boys.

On Saturdays I would go with my mates to the Mayfair picture house in Huyton, where we would see Buster Crabbe, as Flash Gorden, Roy Rogers, Gabby Hayes, and Gene Auntrey. The latter not so popular with the lads because he used sing and kiss the women. Ugh!

We also loved Laurel and Hardy, the Three Stooges and the Bowery Boys.   Some nights I would go with my sister Rosemary to the Regent at Old Swan, the Casino at Fairfield or the Majestic in London Road.   Rosemary would take her ankle socks off outside, to look older to take me in. If that failed we would have to wait and ask people,   " Would you take one in please?" I was due to leave school in the summer of 1955, I was never top of the class but good at history and English and useless at maths.

I always wanted to be a ladies hairdresser. When I told my friends at school they roared with laughter and said that ladies hairdressers were all 'queers' and 'sissies'.

My teacher, Mr Frank Finn said he had an uncle who had a Gent's hairdressers in Prescot, which was a few miles away and he was looking for an apprentice. He arranged an interview so I went with my mother and got the job. The wages were £1=7=6d per week for fifty hours, half day Thursday and no dinner hour on a Saturday if it was too busy.

The shop was called Prices at Kemble Street just by the BICC factory. The first day was spent cleaning the windows, polishing mirrors and cleaning up in general.   Mr Price's son also worked there he had just come out of the R.A.F.

After about four weeks I was taking the sheet off the ones who had finished and brushing them down on the odd occasion a got a 3d tip. I would call the next one, put the taper on the back of his neck, then put the sheet on, if they wanted shaving I would soap their chins.

Then Mr Price would sharpen his open razor on a leather strap and shave them. It was a double fronted shop with three chairs for the customers. I would have a chair ready then brush off the next man who had finished. The customers would sit around the sides and across the windows.

Some weeks later, on a Friday evening after BICC factory closed the shop was so full that men were walking out and not waiting. Father and son were cutting hair and going like the clappers.

" Next please," I shouted. A huge man stood up he was about fifteen stone, with a mop of hair like a Maori, his cap perched I sheeted him up and stood back as usual.

" Right Eddie you start on him", said Mr Price.

" Who me?" I asked with surprise.

""Yes you. Get the wide clippers and start at the back of his neck."

My legs went to jelly, my hands started to shake, I stood behind the man put the clip at the bottom of his neck and pushed up towards the top of his head, the head of the clippers disappeared from view and came out at the crown of his head. There was a gasp from the other customers.

I had cut a two inch path right to the crown of his head the other customers were laughing and nudging each other, lucky for me the customer could not see what I had done. Mr Price turned around to see what they were laughing at.

" Jesus Christ stop, stop! Leave it, leave it, I will finish him."

He finished his customer as fast as he could then come over to take over mine. He had to take the clippers up to keep it even customers were still tittering in the background. The man was bald back and sides with a huge mop on the top so he had to cut that right down as well. The man was not looking too happy and kept looking in the mirror at his head I went over took the sheet off and brushed him off.

He stood up put his cap on and it came down over his eyes and the whole place erupted in laughter, the man was furious.

" I'm not paying for this" he said, pushed past Mr Price and rushed out the shop. Mr Price glared at me,.

" Just brush the bloody floor in future".

Closing time he said, " you're sacked you are not *cut* out for this job!"

My mother always wanted me to get an apprenticeship so I would have a trade at my fingertips.

A few weeks later I got an apprenticeship at A E Lunts at an engineering firm at Kirkby Trading Estate at £2=7=6d per week for a five day week so I could go to the match on a Saturday. Unfortunately they went bankrupt after six months.

David and Brian Bullock who lived next door worked at Crawfords biscuit factory at Edge Lane Liverpool they said that there were some vacancies for boys in the factory or on the vans. I rang up and got an interview and went down a few days later.

There were twelve boys there all aged about fifteen we were interviewed and then shown around the factory. The first place was the tin wash were all the tins were cleaned after returning from the shops In those days, biscuits were sold loose by the pound weight and the tins, which measured approximately 12″ square and returnable.

It was January the place was freezing and these lads were washing rusty tins in cold water, then a fight broke out and there was blood and snot everywhere, hope I don't go in there I thought to myself.

" Come on lads we will go and see the bakery," said the interviewer.

We then went to the packing department and transport department none of the lads fancied the tin wash. We were taken back to the office. Six were taken on and six sent home.

" You two will start in the packing department, you two in the transport department and O'Brien and McNally you start in the tin wash."

We started work at 7.30 am the next Monday, we were given a pair of wellies, a full length rubber apron, a block of white soap and a piece of sacking. There was a big metal tank, which was about 5′ high and 4′ wide. The tins were soaked in this and then lifted out.

The first boy would clean the bottom of the tin then the next four boys would clean a side each with their bits of sacking. The tins would be pushed along a rail and go through a spray of water. If there was dirt or rust left on the tin the big lad at the end would sling it back along the line so you had to be alert in case you got a tin in your face.

I was glad to get the first day over we sat down to our tea a big plate of scouse and did

I need it I was freezing. " How did you get on today Eddie?" mother inquired. " A bit cold Mam but the money is good at £3-2shilling.

The next morning I was dreading getting out of bed, the ice was on the inside of the bedroom window. Outside it was frosty with icy pavements it is going to be freezing cold in the factory today. As I was walking down Binns Road towards the factory I met John McNally.

"How's it going John?"

"I am going to give it a week and see what the score is then, how about you?"

" I will have to stick it out as we need the money".

The foreman, who was about 6 feet tall about 16 stone not one to antagonize was waiting to give his orders.

"Right McNally you stand on that tin then lift them tins out of the tank". John stood on the tin his shoulder level with the top of the tank, which had frozen over during the night.

" Can't get the tins out boss the water is frozen over."

" Well break the fucking ice, you prick".

One of the other boys handed John a metal bar and he smashed the ice up. After half an hour John's hands were going blue with the cold. He had to go deeper in the water to get the tins up. His hands were so cold he could hardly grip the tins.

" You are slowing the line down you little bastard, get a move on".

The tank was filled up again but after another couple of hours John could not continue and the line came to a halt. The foreman ran down to John and kicked the tin from underneath him concrete floor he hurt his elbow, he struggled to his feet.

" Fuck off you big tart you are sacked ".

"Right OBrien, you are on the tank".

Just then the buzzer rang for dinner, thank God for that! After dinner I asked the lad who was filling the tank to keep it topped up so I would not have to reach so far down into the freezing cold water to reach the tins, this was better but it was still very cold, I was glad to get home that night to the warm fire.

I stuck it out for a month, as I wanted to give my Mam a wage at the weekend after all she had done for us. On the Friday night of the fourth week, we had finished work and were taking our wellies and aprons off in the changing rooms one of the big bullies came over and said, holding his foot out,

" Pull my wellies off you little shit".

I said "No". That was fatal, he clenched his fist, I covered my face with my arms and my hands but he punched me hard in the stomach I doubled up on the floor.

" Do you want another one?"

" No, no" I got to me knees and pulled his wellies off tears were coming down my cheeks I tried not to cry in front of the other boys put the pain was too much, every time he saw me he would punch me. I wish I was Rocky Marciano I would give him a hiding he would never forget.

That evening after we had eaten our tea I sat down to watch the television, our new interest. We had only had it a few weeks.

George asked me how it was going at Crawford`s he could see I was not happy. " It`s a bit rough George some of the new lads don`t last a day." He said there was a vacancy at the Whiston Co-Op for an apprentice butcher. Orders were taken out on the bike but there were three half days a week off and the money was about the same as the biscuit factory They are open Saturday morning so give them a ring to make an appointment." I rang up and spoke to a Mr Seddon the Area Manager and got an interview there and then. I caught the number 10 bus at the 'Hole In The Wall' to Prescot I met him at the Prescot shop and he took me along to Warrington Road to another branch, the manager there was Ken O`Brien, no relation. He lived above the shop with his wife and three children.

" When can you start Eddie, we need someone straight away?"

" I can start Monday Ken, if that is alright with you?" Mr Seddan took me back to Prescot and I caught the bus home. I was delighted. When I got home my mother was peeling spuds in the sink.

" I got the job Mam."

She gave me a big hug, " You are not too old to hug your Mum."

I hugged her back. "My boss has the same name as us he is Ken O'Brien he will be a good man as he is a Catholic"

"Don`t bank on it son so was Hitler".

On the Monday I started washing the windows and polishing the rails and weights.

" There are only a few orders this morning, my nephew Kevin will come in and show you where the customers live" said Ken.

There were only about six orders around the Rainhill area, we finished spot on one o`clock. " Before you go Eddie will you put my bet on, take it to Mrs Carrs first house on the right in Brook Street, go around the back."   There were no betting shops then only bookies' runners they had a leather bag with a time lock which had to be locked before the off.   The next morning I was outside waiting for Ken to open up.   After he had finished the window display he made up the orders ready for delivery.

He put them in rotation to make it easier for me, about twenty altogether. My first call was Mrs Dennett of Popular Grove, then Mrs Caine Ash Grove where I got my first cup of tea.

I met a number of elderly people living on their own just wanting to talk.

I was probably the only person they would meet that day. I would never leave my Mam to live like that on her own. A year soon passed. The winters were cold and wet but I loved the job.

I was playing football on Saturdays, Sundays and every chance I got. I was still dreaming of being a footballer. I just lived for my football.

I was an Evertonian. My mate Jimmy Morgan supported Liverpool so he suggested we went to Anfield to watch Liverpool play.

We had never been to Anfield before, and got lost.

We saw a man with a red and white scarf on so we followed him for ages thinking that with the Liverpool colours he would be going to support them. As it turned out, he was going to his mother's house, so we missed the match!

One day a tramp came into the shop he was soaking wet he had two overcoats on tied around the waist with string, a big bushy ginger beard covering his chest.

" Will 2d buy a slice of corned beef son?"

He put the 2d on the counter.

Ken was upstairs. cut him three slices of corned beef and put a meat pie in the bag as well they had been there a week. I gave him the bag and the 2d back.

" Good bless you my son, God bless you."

Then he went on his way. He must have told every tramp in Lancashire as we were getting two to three tramps coming onto the shop every week putting 2d on the counter.

Ken said," Where are all these tramps coming from? We usually only get one every couple of months, have you been treating them?"

" No, one came in for a bone for his dog." I replied feeling guilty.

One Saturday lunchtime, just as we were closing, a couple came into the shop. They told Ken that they had just bought a house around the corner. The man had just left the RAF. He had a handlebar moustache and a badge on his blazer. Ken had also been in the RAF doing his National Service so they were chatting away together.

The woman was younger than him about thirty years of age, slim, dark, very pretty with a huge bust. He bought a piece of beef, then asked for a bone for the dog.

I was scraping the block, " Eddie get a bone for the dog will you a marrow bone and saw it in two."

She came over to the block; I wrapped the bones up and handed them to her. thank you very much" she said and gave me a lovely smile.

They came in the next few Saturdays, I kept some bits for her and cut up a marrowbone and had them ready for her.

" You are a sweetie " She would say, standing right next to me I would blush like mad.

They came in the next Saturday at closing time Ken was talking to the husband, she came over to me by the block.

" That is a big chopper you have got, do you polish it every day?"

"No, only on a Monday!"

"What's your name, mine's Rita."

"Eddie," I croaked nervously.

"Pleased to meet you" she said.

On the way out she told Ken that she might need some meat delivering next week but she would ring first. On the Monday morning I cleaned all the shop it was about 11.a.m.

" Get two pork chops Eddie and take them round the corner to number 5, it's the one with the big tits, take a bone for the dog.

" I took my coat and apron off and walked around to Rita`s
I   went to the side door.

Rita opened the door. "Come in Eddie." She said. I handed her the meat and she put it in the fridge.

" Would you like a cup of tea Eddie, I have just made some. I am afraid we got up late this morning and I'm still in my dressing gown,
Victor has dashed off to work."

" Yes please"

" Well, sit at the table" She handed me a cup of tea and a plate of toast. She sat down facing me, leaning forward her dressing gown opened to the waist. She took a deep breath and her breasts nearly popped out. I missed my mouth with the cup and the tea ran down my chin.

" Here let me wipe your chin with this tissue, you are a slow eater Eddie, I like slow eaters." She was standing very close to me, her breasts swaying side to side, her nipples erect, like two corks my eyes were following them, she got closer.

" Would you like anything else? She shook her breasts from side to side

" Could I have another piece of toast please?"

I asked getting hot under the collar.

" I had better be getting back to the shop."

I ran all the way back to the shop. " Where the hell have you been?" "
She kept me talking for ages," was all I could stammer.

Victor and Rita both came in the next Saturday. Ken was upstairs so I served them they bought a piece of pork and a bone for the dog.

" Where do you go for your lunch Eddie?" Victor asked.

"I usually go to the chippie in Prescot."
" Well why don't you come and have lunch with us on Monday it will save you going to Prescot?"
" Thank you very much Victor."
" You are very welcome Eddie" said Rita with a big smile.
On Monday morning Rita rang up for three large lamb chops, I took them to their house. Rita opened the door " Come in Eddie the tea is made."   She
wore skin tight jeans and a white sweater her nipples bursting through.
I drank my tea.   Rita
said," I will see you at lunch time Eddie I will be waiting for you."
" Okay Rita I'll see you later."
I arrived spot on 1 p.m. Victor opened the door.
" Come in Eddie we will sit in the lounge while Rita prepares lunch."
The house was like a palace, fitted carpets, drape curtains, cocktail cabinet, just like you see on the pictures.
" Sit on the settee Eddie, lunch is nearly ready, would you like a glass of wine."
" I don't drink Victor."
" It is only wine, not very strong." He poured three glasses of red wine, handed me one and took one out to Rita.
" It wont be long now Eddie." He sat in the armchair. Rita came in carrying her empty glass, she had a loose fitting flowery dress on.
" Give us a top up darling, drink up Eddie, don`t be shy."
Victor topped the glasses up to the brim. Rita sat next to me on the settee. " How old are you Eddie?" " fifteen nearly siteen."
" That's a nice age, you have a lot of learning to do."
" I'll serve lunch now," she said as she went into the kitchen. After a few minutes she called us into the dinning room. Victor sat at one end, Rita and I facing each other at either side. There was just a lamb chop on the plate. " Help yourself to potatoes, vegetables and gravy.
At home everything was piled on the plate, they must be very posh I thought.
Victor filled our glasses again. " That was a lovely meal Rita."
" You are more than welcome Eddie." She said with a wink and a smile.
We went back to sit in the lounge Rita sat next to me on the settee.
Victor went and put his coat on and said he had to get back to the office.
" Cheerio Eddie, bye-bye darling."
He kissed Rita on the cheek and departed. Rita filled my glass up again.
My head was spinning. " You are very mature for your age Eddie and

handsome. Is the wine getting to you?"

" No, no, no" I spluttered, "I am fine." I could hardly see .

She moved closer to me. " Do you know Victor never takes me out and is useless in bed, he's not interested in me I think he was a *rear gunner* in the R.A.F! if you know what I mean" She put her hand on my thigh I think she was getting giddy.

"Excuse me I will have to go to the toilet," I spluttered.

I wanted to try and clear my head. Good job it was my half- day off. When I came downstairs, she had her hand up her dress scratching herself, and moaning. I thought, "I hope she's not got fleas!" She leaned back on the cushion; she pulled the dress up to her waist, her legs apart. God she has no knickers on.

" Come here Eddie".   She undid my trousers and they fell to the floor, she took hold of my little willie, it felt good,

I thought this is better than going to the chippie!

I looked down, it looked like a birds nest between her legs, she pulled me down on top of her.

How do you get in? I had never seen one before. I was prodding away without success, then she got hold of my little willie and shoved it in. It was heaven, better than football.

She was panting and moaning, I don't think I lasted long enough for her, about ten seconds, as she started to *scratch* herself again. Rita started to moan and groan. Maybe she is having a fit That was my first sexual encounter. I will never forget it.

A couple of months later I was moved to another branch of The CO-OP at Whiston Village. There was a pub called the Horseshoe Inn, a post office, a couple of small shops and a Labour Club and that was it. There were two butchers in the shop, both in their 30`s, Harry and Fred both friendly and cheerful like most butchers, Harry was of medium height with grey hair and a ruddy complexion. He smoked a pipe and looked a bit of a 'smoothie'. Fred was an ugly bastard, tall, thin and gaunt, his hair parted in the middle, a chain smoker

Things were laid back in the Co-op, Harry would go over to the pub a couple of afternoons in the week and have a game of bowls, or have a liquid lunch. He'd come back and start dancing with the customers it was more like Butlins.

I soon settled in, there were a lot more deliveries and being a rural area it was very pleasant in the summer. The Co-op staff had their own internal bartering system, the butcher would give the grocer free meat, likewise with the Co-op milkman, coal man and bread man and they would all return the favour with their own goods. No money changed hands, there were thousands of Co-op shops all over the country, and if you spent a pound they would give you 2/6d back as divi.

You could imagine the cost of the bartering system all over the country. All the managers had new cars, but they were only on £10 a week, they would change their cars often.

Getting the same make model and colour so no one would notice.

The Co-op was the Socialists' dream that went down the pan because of fiddlers. Monday morning I cleaned all the shop.

Harry and Fred got all the orders ready to take, I put them in rotation, then Harry said," Give me Mrs Merton`s order, I will take that one."

He put the parcel inside his apron and got into his blue Gordon three wheeler car and sped off.

" That's his bit on the side, Eddie." Fred said.

I set off through the village down to Huyton Quarry then as far as Rainhill, quite a good run out.

Harry took Mrs Merton`s order twice a week and apparently, she would open the door with just her bath towel around her then she would run back into the large through lounge. Harry would chase her around the coffee table then he'd dive on her and give her a good seeing to on the carpet! Unknown to Harry, the neighbours had been watching them for weeks, as everybody knew it was Harry's car as it was always parked outside the shop.

So four of the young neighbours went upstairs in the house opposite to get a grandstand view. That afternoon the four women came into the shop to tease Harry.

Harry was boning out on the block, Fred was serving, they were all young mothers from the estate.

" Did Mrs Merton get her sausage this morning?" one of them shouted. Harrys face went crimson. " Did you get your chopper out?" they were all shouting and roaring with laughter.

" We watched you this morning, shagging her on the carpet."

Harry dashed into the back room. He never went again!

Mrs Merton was not liked in the close were they lived, she was only in her early twenties with a stunning figure.

As her husband worked away the other men in the close offered to cut her lawn and do odd job for her, which did not go down well with their wives. On the Thursday I put all the orders into the basket including Mrs Merton`s. Harry said nothing. I flew around and could not wait to get to Mrs Merton`s. She opened the door in her dressing gown.

" Come in, would you like a brew?" She sauntered over to put the kettle on, her bum swaying from side to side. I could feel my little willie twitching, she swayed back, her breasts fighting to get out of her dressing gown, she stood in front of me her breasts nearly touching. She said in a slow sexy voice," Could you do something for me?
I held my breath.
"Could you pass me that cup out of the cupboard".
I had my cup of tea, then continued my round. The next day we were sitting in the back of the shop studying the racing paper, it seemed that most butchers like a bet on the horses.
Fred and Harry started to talk about motorbikes as they both had one when they were younger. I said that my brother George had a Norton Dominator, 500cc and I would like one when I got older, If I could save up enough money.
Harry said winking at Fred that Mrs Merton had one in her shed at home, with her husband working away most of the time it was just lying there he said and it would be sold pretty cheap
"What do you think Eddie?"
" I do not know depends how much it is."
Fred said, " Give her a ring Harry, say that it's for Eddie our apprentice."
Harry rang Mrs Merton "Hello Kate you know that old motorbike you have in the shed young Eddie here wants to buy it, maybe you could give him a ride."
"He can have a ride alright make it 1 o`clock tomorrow I will be ready for him."
They both started to laugh. That evening I told George about the motorbike he said that he`d come and pick me up at 1 o`clock and he would have a look at it for me.
He came down next day and we roared off down the road on his Norton to Mrs Merton`s, we stopped outside her house I got off and walked up the path to the side door while George was taking his helmet off and putting the bike on the stand. I knocked on the door, Mrs Merton opened the door she was naked; the only thing she had on was the radio. My mouth fell open.
" Come in Eddie."
" Oh, oh, my brother is here as well." He put her head around the door. George was walking up the path.
" The bike is in the shed." She then slammed the door shut. We looked in the shed where there was an old motorbike. It had flat tyres and did not even have telescopic forks. It was a wreck George dropped me back

at the shop.

" Waste of time that, Eddie, I will see you later. " he said and then he roared off back to work.

I went into the back of the shop, Fred and Harry were just getting their coats and aprons on, they were grinning all over their faces.

Harry said," What did you ride Eddie, Kate or the motorbike?" They both roared laughing, the bastards had set me up.

Monday morning came and I was putting the orders in the basket.

" Watch that Kate does not get a grip of you Eddie".

Harry shouted as I was going out the door, I dashed around as fast as I could to get to Kate's. I was about to knock on the door when I saw a note saying please put the meat in the shed. Same thing on Thursday I felt really miserable. On the following Monday no note, I knocked on the door, Kate opened the door," Come in Eddie would you like a cup of tea?" ·

"Yes please, Kate". She put the meat in the fridge and then put the kettle on, I was standing leaning against the kitchen unit, she came over to me, her dressing gown was open. She had white knickers on but no bra.   She leaned against me, put her arms around my neck and gave me a long, lingering kiss, she undid my zip and fondled me, she went down one knee and took my willie out and put it in her mouth, moving slowly back and forth, it was ecstasy.

On the following Thursday, I knocked on the door full of trepidation, I was about to step in but there was a man standing there, I handed him the meat.

" Thank you very much," On the following Monday, Kate answered the door and said her husband was home for two weeks. On the Monday I put the orders in rotation, no meat for Kate.

" Have you forgotten Kate's meat Harry?"

" No she is coming in for it herself."

I got back a fast as I could so I could see Kate in the shop, she came in at 12.55, just before closing, she looked stunning, she had a white crossover top on and a bare midriff her, breasts bulging over the top and skin tight white trousers.

The other customers had left the shop leaving only Kate in the shop. Fred locked the door then he went over for his liquid lunch at the Horseshoe pub. Harry and I went into the back of the shop Kate followed us through.

Harry handed me a five pound note, "Eddie, go and get some fish and chips and take your time, I have to talk to Kate."

I went out the back door and around to the chippie, there was a queue but I was in not in a hurry got to give Harry time to chat to Kate.

By the time I got back 25 minutes had elapsed.

I opened the back door, Harry had Kate stripped naked except for her boots, what a body. She was lying on the block with her legs over his shoulders, he was pounding away like a man possessed.

He looked over his shoulder as I came in, " Shut the fucking door quick" Kate smiled. I went over and put the kettle on not knowing what to do. He was going like the clappers her breasts were bouncing like two big jellies.

" Did you get the mushy peas Eddie?"

" Yes, Harry,"

"Do you take sugar, Kate?"

"Yes please Eddie, oh my God I am coming" she screamed.

Harry collapsed on top of her. That was good Kate."

He bent down and pulled his trousers up.

"Do us a chip buttie Eddie, please " said Kate. She stood there naked just her boots on she bent over to pull her nickers up

Harry shafted her again she screamed "Fuck ,fuck get it right in any hole".

I thought wish I could have go.

We all sat down as though it was an every day occurrence.

After we had finished eating Kate asked Harry if her meat was ready.

" What would you like?"

" Cumberland sausage."

We all burst out laughing.

Harry could not go down to Kate`s house so she would pick it up at the shop at lunchtime, then she would get a good seeing to.

Harry would give me a pound to go over to the pub for a meat pie and half of bitter he said, " And don`t not come back until 2.15, you little pervert"

I was at that shop for another six months, still football mad and no steady girlfriend . I used to go with my mates to Liverpool town centre clubs the Mardi Gras , Grafton, Locarno, the Pink Parrot, Dutch Eddie`s and the Temple Bar in Dale Street. By now I was 18 years old. With all of us in the family working, we enjoyed a good standard of living.

No more holes in our shoes, no more dripping butties, no need for Sturlas or Colliers clothing cheques. My mother could buy herself a nice pinny or dress.   It was probably the happiest period of my mother`s life but it was not to last. I had been in bed a couple of hours I was woken up.

"Eddie get up quickly," My sister Rosemary was shaking me,,
" Mam is not too good, come downstairs." I got dressed and hurried
down to the front room, my mother was sitting in the armchair, her
head leaning on her chest. She was having difficulty breathing, George
was kneeling at her side holding her hand.

Rosemary said, " I have called the doctor, they said he is on his way, but
that was twenty minutes ago, I had better call again, get Ginny Privalege
to come in. "

Rosemary was back in ten minutes with Ginny and her daughter-in-law
Peggy.

Rosemary said, "Dr Imundy is on his way, his surgery is only a couple of
miles away in Bluebell Lane.

Another ten minutes passed, Ginny said, "How long is it since you called
the doctor Rosemary."

" It must be over half an hour since the first call, just after midnight.
Ginny handed Peggy some coppers for the phone box.

"You go Peggy and tell him to get down here fast."

Mother was hardly breathing now, her false teeth were hanging out of
her mouth, wish someone would take then out. Ginny leaned over and
gently took them out,.

Peggy came back "He is on his way."

" They have been saying that for the last hour" retorted Ginny.

A couple more neighbours came in.

" I am going to call an ambulance." Ginny rushed out to the phone box.

The ambulance took about ten minutes to arrive, still no doctor.

They came in and examined my mother and said, " I am afraid she is
dead, there is no pulse. "

Just then the doctor came rushing in, he confirmed that she was dead,
the ambulance men left.

Ginny turned on the doctor, " You took your bleeding time, didn`t you,
over one hour to come three miles!"

" I was out on other calls."

" Out on the bleeding tiles, more like it you jewish bastard"

The doctor said it was a cerebral haemorrhage and he could not have
saved her anyway, then left.

There were about ten people in the room now; nobody seemed to know
what to do

Rosemary, George and myself just embraced each other sobbing our
hearts out just stunned.

Ginny said," It would be better if we brought a single bed down and laid her on the bed."

Tony, Ginny`s son, went and brought the bed down and put it under the window,,

" You and Eddie get her legs George."

Tony beckoned a neighbour over, John. "John and I will get her shoulders."

My mother was so heavy we struggled to get her out of the armchair, I could hardly see the tears were tripping me up.

We lifted her out of the chair, just got to the end of the bed and we dropped her on the floor.

Is there a God? Some other people came over to help us and we managed to lay her on the bed. The neighbours went into the back kitchen and put the kettle on, and sat around and chatted. I felt I wanted to get out of the house to think, I went outside and sat on the step, just outside the front door.

I was angry with the doctor who had kept saying he was on his way.

I hated God who had taken my lovely mother after all she had been through, we were just getting on our feet and then he takes her away. If I was God, there would be no suffering in the world, nobody would die, there would be no cancer or children dying of starvation, no racism, no poverty, everyone would be happy and love one another. If I were God, I would have that power. LIKE THIS GOD HAS THE POWER NOW!

The next morning the undertakers arrived and laid my Mam in an open coffin with a large crucifix on the lid, which was standing up against the wall.

After they had left, Rosemary said, " We should go in and see her together."   Rosemary hesitated with her hand on the doorknob, George put his hand over hers, turned the knob and we went in.

She looked so lovely and peaceful, the worry lines seemed to have gone, she was sixty one years old, no age to die.

Some of the neighbours had brought mass cards.

Rosemary placed them around the sides of the coffin, we just stood there and cried, just could not believe what was happening.

Then we thought of poor Allen out in Tripoli doing his National Service with the Irish Rangers, thousands of miles away, there would be no one to console him.

George contacted the army but they said owing to the distance, he could not get any compassionate leave.

My Mothers death hurt so much I was getting pains in my stomach, over the next day or two I would go in on my own and hold her hand, talk to her, tell her how much I loved her, how much I miss her, she was the best Mam in the world

My mother was buried with Little Joseph and my father a terrible day. I would go for out for a drink in the Bluebell Inn I would come home then it would hit me a silent empty house. "WHERE ARE YOU MAM" I would run up and down the stairs shouting for her but no reply. If you have a mother look after her because you won't get another one.

With not having a father I became so close to my mother, she was my Idol, my best mate.

It is now 1958. A few months later I am moved to the main shop at Eccleston Street Prescot. I bade my farewells to Harry, Fred and Kate; we had had some laughs together.

The manager at Prescot was Ernie Edwards, a big man, must have weighed 18 stones, probably more. He used to smoke Capstan Full Strength. He was a chain smoker, there were nicotine stains all around his lips, in fact, and he used to serve my mother years before at the Co-op butchers near our house at Huyton.

It was just after the war. My mother had bought a breast of lamb and " Ernie, have you any bones for the dog?" and little Allen said,
" Are we getting a dog mam?"

There was another butcher there at Prescot called Bill Critchley but he did not stay long. The shop was not very busy there, the likes of Lennons and Dewhurst with their full window displays left the Co-op behind. Anything socialist stays in a time warp. All we had in the window was a bowl of dripping and two pigs livers.

I was well into backing horses every day, I was on a roll, I would study form for hours then stick to my own formula. I would look at the 2 o'clock races, if they were sprints and had a clear favourite say, even money to 4-1, I would back £5 to win, if cash £10 to win up and down plus a £5 double. If one of the horses was number 7 I would double the stakes, If they were top weight in the handicap I would back them each way, number 7 was my lucky number.

I was invited to Chester Race Course by a couple, he was Alex Bicket ex Co-op man, he had left the Co-op and opened his own shop, and his wife Brenda who was second man on the bacon slicer when she was at the Co-op. I had never been to a racecourse before so I was really excited. We both backed a couple of donkeys,
" I thought you were good at this game, Eddie"
" I usually am, I must have lost my touch today, I fancy Yellow Sovereign

in the next race. The 3.30 Joe Mercer is on, it is 100 to 8."
I put £5 each way Alec backed the favourite it was a close finish. Yellow Sovereign came third but I am sure if Joe Mercer had tried a little harder it would have won. I thought I would keep an eye on it next time out. I only bet in pounds if I was winning,
I used to pick 5 horses and do 5 x yanks for 27/6d 55bets in all.
Every thursday on my half day, I would go in to Liverpool just to bet. I would have a few pints in the Temple in Dale Street then go to the betting shop in Cheapside I looked in the morning paper, I saw that Yellow Sovereign was running in the 4 o`clock at Doncaster.
I thought that I would go mad and back £20 each way. I jumped on the number 10 bus and got off at the bottom of Low Hill, I thought for a change I would go to the Swan betting shop there. It was only 2.p.m so I had two hours to kill before the 4.p.m race.   I
started to look at runners for the earlier races. I thought I would have a little bet while I was waiting. 3.30 came I had lost the £40.
As I walked out the man behind the counter shouted, " Come again son, glad to see you" .He was taking the piss.
I walked down London Road toward Pembroke Place, stupid bastard.
Then I thought, nothing ventured, nothing gained, so I went in the post office at Pembroke Place and drew £40 out of my savings account, dashed back to the betting shop and put £20 each way on Yellow Sovereign. It walked it, winning by three lengths at 100-6. I had won about £450, I waited until they had weighed in and went to the counter for my winnings. He was not laughing now. " I will call again mate, glad to see you" and I threw him a £5 note. "Have a pint mate."
I think in your lifetime you have one run of luck and I was having mine. I was winning nearly everyday, about £200 a week. My boss, Ernie asked why don`t I pack my job in and just do the horses, I was running back and forth to the betting shop all afternoon.
Ernie had a mate who had a sweet and tobacco shop just around the corner, he was in the shop telling Ernie he had lost a packet on the horses, I had just walked in from the back of the shop.
"Here is the man you want, Eddie can not go wrong at the moment, talk to him."
That day I gave him two winners. Over the next three weeks I gave him six winners, good prices, not favourites.
Ernie said, "My mate had won a fortune from your tips as he backed heavily. Has he treated you? "
" How do you mean?"

" Has he give you a bung, you know a couple of quid?"
" No I have had nothing." Ernie must of have a word because when he came to the shop next time he came over.
" That is for you Eddie, my pal. " He put his hand in his pocket and handed me a white paper sweet bag.
" Thank you very much." I tucked the sweet bag in my apron, I went into the back of the shop, I squeezed the bag, there must be a good wad in there, I opened it, inside was twenty woodbines in an open top packet The tight bastard I thought. I had two horses for him that day so I changed for two donkeys; I went back into the shop.
" Here you are John two certs for you today, put plenty on."
He came back next day, fuming, " I lost a packet yesterday, they came nowhere."
" I have got a cracker for you today John, it is called "Th Boggart", its due for a win, it's a good outsider, you will clean up."
Th` Boggart" came nowhere. He never came back again.
Within eighteen months George, Rosemary and Allen all got married, it` funny how things can change so quickly in less than two years. There was mother, George, Allen and Rosemary and myself sitting around the table having our meals together, now there was just me.
I felt abandoned and very lonely. I got moved again to a shop at Hillside Road, Huyton, just a few minutes away from home, the manager was an odd bod from Wigan, what we would call a woollie back. I arrived on my bike at 8.a.m and was surprised to see the window laid out full of trays of various meat. " You might well look, I have been here since 7a.m."
" Well I get paid from 8a.m. so that is when I start, all right."
I put my bike in the back of the shop I thought that is a good start to the day. The first customer did not come in till after 9 o`clock then a part time assistant came in at 10a.m., a large middle aged lady called Mrs Cowen.
She was very nice and welcoming,
"What is his problem?"
" He is always like that, miserable bugger."
A few days later I was talking to the man himself, Jim Barton, we were having our tea break at the back of the shop,.
" I suppose you being a Catholic support Everton having all those mick's playing for them." " I do support Everton not because I am a Catholic, religion hs nothing to do with it, my brother supports Liverpool,
I suppose you support Wigan Rugby League Club, because you are a pie eater." End of conversation .

Wigan people hate being called pie eaters, because in the 1926 General Strike the Wigan miners were first to give in and go back to work, so they ate humble pie and they have never lived it down.

The Scousers were last to go back.

I was having my tea one evening, it was Summer 1959 and there was a loud knocking on the door.

It was Mrs Lynch who lived further down the road, she was in an agitated state.

"Could you come Eddie and see how Francis is? She has locked herself in the back kitchen and I can't get in."

Francis lived next door but one, she was the one who informed the council when we were selling lemonade from the house. I climbed over the back fence and gingerly opened the back door, there was a smell of gas,

Francis was sitting on a stool her head in the gas oven on a cushion.

" Are you alright Francis?" Daft thing to say looking back, there was no reply.   I put my arms under her shoulders and lifted her up, her head fell back looking up at me, her face looked swollen, black and blue, she had no teeth in.   I dragged her out to the back garden and laid her on the ground. She was obviously dead. The police and ambulance came and I made a statement. A few weeks later, someone had been in touch with the council to tell them I was living in a three bedroomed house on my own. I had just received a letter from the council saying that there were family`s who needed my house and I would have to find somewhere else but they would give me 28 days notice. It is good is it not?   Your family pay rent for twenty years and then you are kicked out.

A woman came into the shop who I knew from the church club, I was telling her about my predicament, and she said one of her neighbours had been in the same situation and had advertised her house in the Liverpool Echo to exchange for a private house. As long as the people were on the housing list you could swap.

I put an ad in the Echo and got about 20 replies, I went to see a couple of houses in Anfield, one house was so filthy I had to wipe my feet coming out. The third house I went to see was 45 Imison Street Breeze Hill, Walton. It was a two up and two down, no bathroom, outside toilet.

I got quite a surprise when the woman opened the door.

She was a former neighbour called Finnegan she had lived with her mother in the next road to me, Parbrook Road, Huyton, she said she had two children and wanted the extra bedroom and bathroom plus she wanted to be back near her mother.

She said if I paid her mortgage off, about £100 and legal fees, we could do a straight swop. She was on the council waiting list so there was no problem, so we went ahead.   She was delighted getting a family house on low rent. I thought I would rent it out. I decorated the house and furnished it with decent second hand furniture.

I used an accommodation bureau in Liverpool they found tenants and vetted them, they sent down a young nurse called Diane Marshall who said that she worked at Blackburn Royal Infirmary and that she had worked there five years. I met her outside the house, she was blonde, very attractive, looked like a young Barbara Windsor.

I showed her around. She said she was moving from Blackburn to Walton Hospital in Liverpool, which was just a few minutes away. She liked the house and she paid me a months rent in advance, £32. I asked her to pay the next rent straight into my bank.

I was quite pleased with myself. This landlord job was a piece of cake. I rang up Blackburn Infirmary and they confirmed that a Miss Diane Marshall worked there.

The first month soon passed, I checked with my bank, Nat West at Old Swan, no rent had been paid in. I went down to the house, knocked on the door but there was no answer. The man from next door, came out, "They have left a few days ago, a big furniture van, and my son-in-law's push bike was in the back of the van." I got such a shock that went over my head. I opened the door, the place had been stripped bare, even the carpet that I had nailed to the floor and the sink was missing. I went around to Breeze Hill police station that was just around the corner. D.S. Liddel from C.I.D took me into a side room I explained what had happened,

"Not that blonde again, you are the fourth landlord in the last couple of months she has robbed, she is a front for a professional gang, they rent houses then go to the big furniture store in town, get the best G-plan furniture on H.P also TV`s, radiogram and cookers.

Your furniture is just a bonus, she uses a false name someone who is working that you can check on, I don't hold out much hope of catching them. "

I put the house on the market; I gave it to Blake's Estates Agents in Old Swan. They put it on the market at £900 and they soon found a buyer at £850,I was glad to see the back of it.

A friend of my brother George came to see me called Phil Tongue he had a butchers shop in Market Street Prescot. He had opened another one in

Garston and he had put his brother in to run it but things had not worked out. He offered to rent it to me at £7 per week including a flat above the shop. I accepted. I gave my notice in at the Co-op and moved into the flat, the shop had been closed for a couple of weeks but it had done well in the past.

I bought a new Austin a40 Farina estate car from Llewellyns in Whitechapel it was red with a black roof I could pick my meat up in it from Stanley Abattoir I arranged to meet Phil Tongue at 6.30 am, he said he would give me a idea what meat to buy to open the shop with I spent the first day giving the place a good clean out.

I opened up the following morning, which was Tuesday. The shop was at 90 Window Lane. There was a lot of passing trade going to work in the factories and the Garston Bottle Works, which had a large work force. The first month was very slow, and then it started to pick up. If I did not sell most of the stock I would not have any wages, all the money was in unsold meat, which was in the fridge

There was a young Geordie policeman who kept popping in for cups of tea his name was Mike. I had been over to the Woodcutters Club just across the road; I had had a good session and was having a little difficulty getting the key in the front door.

"Look out give it to me" I looked around it was Mike the local bobby, he opened the door " Pissed again Ed"

"No just merry"

"Are you putting the kettle on Ed"

"No I am knackered Mike, you help yourself, put some sausage on if you want, put the keys through the letterbox when you go, it is nearly midnight I am off to bed, good night Mike "Good night Ed."

The following Monday I picked my meat up at Stanley Abattoir at 7a.m. Turned left towards Old Swan then a right turn into Broadgeen Road by the Red House pub.

When I came to the first intersection a black ford Zephyr came out of the side road at about 50 miles an hour smashed right into my passenger side, the impact pushed me onto two wheels. I was now on the wrong side of the road and a double decker bus was bearing down on me. There were eggs flying all over the place. Luckily I got back on four wheels slammed on the brakes and stopped a few feet from the bus, a couple of people helped me out I could hardly stand up I was unhurt but badly shaken. The Ford Zephyr had driven back into the side street. Four big black gentlemen got out and came over. The one I took to be the driver said "Sorry man I have just come over from Somaliland and I can't tell the side roads from the main roads".

"I will have to call the Police".

"Please don't I have no road tax or insurance, I will pay for the damage to your car, if you bring your car down to my house tonight at 11 Upper Parliament Street, Toxteth I will give you the name and address of a garage that will repair your car".

I agreed I took his registration number and got a few names and addresses as witnesses, for insurance purposes. I went around to the police station but they were not interested because no one was injured. That evening I went around to see Mr Mot the black gentleman at Toxteth, the it was a large house split into flats, I knocked on the door, a tall black chap answered it.

"Is Mr Mo in?" "No there is nobody here by that name"

He looked the image of Mr Mot, he was some relation Tell Mr Mot when he comes in if he is not down at my address in the morning I am going to the police. The next morning at 10 am a green ford Zehpyr pulled up outside the shop all the back was smashed in as well. Mr Mot came in. I am sorry about the mix up last night my brother thought you were the police, here is the address of the garage that will repair your car it is in Back Canning Street.

I took the car down at lunch time, I was not very impressed it was a bit of a shed with cars and parts all over the place. I left the car the black gentleman said he would have to order a new door and he would ring me when it was ready. I waited three weeks no call so I rang the garage, he said the car was ready but he had not been paid yet, so I could not pick it up I rang him a week later success he had been paid, I went down and picked the car up on Wednesday my half day, I arrived back at the shop, waiting there for his cup of tea was Mike the bobby, I am glad to get it back Mike, I had had to get my meat delivered by Suckling Transport it cost a fortune

I walked around the car and stood next to Mike on the pavement he was staring at the passenger door.

"Just a minute Eddie that door looks a lighter red than the rest of the car".

I stepped back, "I think your are right Mike, there is a slight difference, .I am not going to take it back there they will another couple of weeks

"Put the kettle on Eddie."

"That is all you worry about is your bloody tea".

I was still not making any money out of the shop I was living and eating but not making wages

A few months later the Garston bottle works closed down and a few of the smaller factories and I lost all my passing trade, a few months later I closed the shop and stayed in the flat to take stock of the situation. I had signed a 12 months lease so I had no choice.

On the following Sunday I had made arrangements to meet my mate George Caldwell in the Beehive pub in Liverpool town centre at 7.30 p.m. I was approaching town driving along Park Road, on my right there were crowds coming out of ST Patrick's church on the corner. People were lining the pavement waiting to cross when suddenly a little girl about seven or eight made a dash across the road right in front of me. I braked as hard as I could but hit her head on, she went up in the air like a rag doll, and she came down onto my bonnet then slid down onto the road.

The crowds swarmed around the car banging on the windows shouting, "You mad bastard you were going to fast."

I thought it best to stay were I was I did not think I was going to fast as was in a line of traffic, luckily the police and ambulance were her in no time just a few minutes I was glad to see them as I thought I was going to be lynched When I got out of the car I could her the little girl crying so I new she was not dead.

I was standing at the back of the car answering police questions when this big man came over I was expecting a smack in the eye, but he said in a Irish accent

"I saw the whole thing officer this man did all he could to stop but the girl ran out in front of him nobody could have stopped. The police put me in the back of the police car as some of the crowd was still hostile. The police measured the road then made out a report this took about forty five minutes they gave me a ticket to produce my documents, the crowd had dispersed. I asked the policeman what hospital she would have been taken to so I could see how she was, he radioed through and after about ten minutes he found that the girl was back at home with just a few bruises he gave me her address it was just around the corner. I went around to her house her mother opened the door .

"I am the driver." I was wondering what reception I was going to get.

"Come in she is in the front room."

She was lying on the settee, a bandage on her head and one on her knee.   "I am very sorry I did my best to avoid you."

"It was my own fault I should have waited"

There was no malice at all I stayed for half an hour and had a cup of tea. I took documents to Garston police station and heard no more about it

Did this car have a jinx on it I never bought another red car I rang my mate up at the Beehive and explained what happened and that I was going to have an early night.

The next morning at 11 a.m. there a knock on the front door, it is Mike the bobby,   "Morning Eddie get the kettle on lad."

"You're a cheeky bastard don't people miss you when you go missing half of the time?"

"It is better on nights I keep a look out for women who live on there own or husband's on the night shift, if there is a light on after midnight I knock and asked is everything alright, usually I get invited in for a cup of tea and anything else that is on offer, sometimes I get my truncheon out".

"I you bet you do".

After Mike had gone I decided to go into to town to see if I could recapture my winning streak on the horses, I went into my old haunt the betting shop in Cheapside off Dale Street I put £2 win on the first two favourites in the 2.00 races and a £2 double both unplaced I had that gut feeling that I was not going to win so if in doubt bail out. I looked at a bit more form and decided to go across to the Temple bar and have a pint, there standing at the bar was an old school mate of mine Joe Gatt I had not seen him for years he lived in our road and went to the same school.

"All right Joe".

"Alright Ed God! I have not seen you for years, are you still a butcher?"

"Unemployed butcher at the moment Joe," I explained about the shop

"What are you up to then Joe you were always a fly bastard."

He laughed "I have calmed down now Ed since leaving Huyton, I am a grill chef at the Shaftesbury Hotel, loads of young girls there, I am fighting them off.

We talked about school day old mates who we had seen and had not seen, then the tale about his auntie Mary, he must have told me this tale about a dozen times, His auntie Mary lived across the road in Pennard Ave just after the war there was a shortage of most things particularly ladies stocking girls used to put leg tan on or draw a black line down the back their legs so it would look like a seam, His auntie Mary had a brain wave she put gravy browning on her legs and she had all the dogs chasing her down the street trying to lick her legs.

We had a couple more pints then Joe had to start work

"I am off now Eddie do you fancy going to the baths at Dovecote tomorrow?"

"Yes that would be great Joe, I will pick you up at 2 p.m. He told me his address 27 Moscow Drive Stoneycroft Liverpool.

We used to go to Dovecot baths when we were at St Columba's School the whole class would go about 40 of us we would arrive at 3.30 p.m. then had to be out by 4.p.m. the teacher Mr Dooley would wait until we were nearly dressed then he would go home we would get undressed again put our wet cozzies on and go back in.

We spent a couple of hours at the baths. We had a pint at the Knotty Ash Hotel then back to Joe's flat, were we had had coffee and a sandwich we had a good chat about the old days about 4.m the phone went is was the hotel wanting Joe to go in as somebody had not turned in.   Joe said he would have to go but would I hang on until 5p.m. because one of his girlfriends was coming and would I explain what had happened.

"Watch yourself with this one Eddie she is sex on legs, she can't get enough, do anything she had a gang bang one afternoon in the hotel her name is Gina

The doorbell went at 5p.m. Gina stood there she was absolutely gorgeous

"Come in, Joe has had to go into work someone has not turned in he said he would see you later". She took her coat off her figure was breathtaking, more than an ample bust her dress was as tight as her skin, an arse you could eat.

"I had better be going now Gina. "

Don't go I am just about to make some coffee, what's you name?"

"Eddie"

"Come on Eddie a quick cup of coffee wont hurt."

I did not need much persuading, "O.K. Gina I will have a coffee with you" I sat on the settee she brought the coffee over and sat next to me.

"I am going to North Wales next week to Talacre in my mates caravan, have you been there Eddie ?

"No I have been to Bala and Barmouth but not Talacre."

"Here, I will show you on the map." She got up and took a map out of the sideboard draw, spreading it across our knees she started to circle were she thought Talacre was hovering over my twitching willie, pressing down as she circled with her finger.

"Sorry Gina I have to go I have a doctors appointment at 6.30 in Mount Pleasant". I have been having trouble with my back it had given me a lot of pain and I could not move when it started to size up.

After the doctor examined me he said it could be with handling cold meat all the time as he had known fishmongers having the same problem, he gave me some pain killers. I started to look around for a job, I made a appointment for Burtons the Tailors for11 A.M. the next morning.

As I was walking down Church Street I spotted Gina on the other side of the coming towards me I shouted her and she came over she was dabbing her eyes with a hankerchief.

".What is wrong Gina?"

"I have been to my solicitor to finalize my divorce, I am crying more with relief than sorrow, he was a right bastard used to knock shit out of me he was a piss artist when I was 7 months pregnant he pushed me down the stairs and I lost the baby and I can't have anymore".

"You must have married very young".

"Yes when I was 17 almost 3 years ago"

Sod the interview I thought, I had better look after this girl we went for a coffee in the Wimpy Bar she told me about all the trouble she had had with her ex husband, after about half an hour .

"Would you like to come back to my penthouse if you have nothing on, I mean nothing to do?"

"I would love to Eddie I feel better already."

As I pulled up outside the shop we had just got out the car when a familiar voice said, " Put the kettle on Eddie" it was Mike the bobby, he must hide around the corner

" Sorry Mike I am a bit busy at the moment."

"I can see that" he leaned over and whispered in my ear " two`s up Eddie"

" Piss off"

I opened the door as we were going upstairs "what did he say?"

"He said two`s up"

"I have never had a copper before"

"Just get up the stairs" We went into the lounge

" Jesus this is more like a shit house than a penthouse, when did you last clean up?"

" It is only a bit of dust, I had to sack the maid, you know how it is, do you want another coffee?"

" No thanks, get your trousers off, the thought of that copper has got me going, I like men in uniform, especially with big helmets"

We kissed passionately our tongues tantalizing each other, I could fell her breasts hardening under my caress, her hands went down to my zip.

"Let us get into the bedroom",

She stopped and said she could not get undressed in front of anyone she

would like to go in first, get stripped and get into bed.
I took my clothes off and waited. " Coming ready or not"
I got into bed he had the most wonderful body I had ever seen, not that
I'd seen many, we kissed passionately our tongues entwined. I licked her
nipples, her breasts were hard as rock.
"That was great Eddie, now fuck me stupid".
"Who are you calling stupid?"
"Stick it in"
And I thought romance was dead She rolled up like a contortionist her
feet either side of her head, I mounted her, I was thrusting away when a
hand grasped my balls from the back, I looked around, thought someone
had come in.
She rang me a few days later, she said she had left the hotel and got a
job at Knotty Ash petrol station, she finished at five o'clock and asked
could I pick her up as she had a large bag of shopping. She suggested we
go back to my penthouse and she would cook the tea and have a bottle
of wine. After a lovely meal we went straight to bed, she was definitely
cock happy, she stayed over night and when I woke up she had left for
work,   I felt as thought I had run a marathon twice.
Later that afternoon   Joe rang, he wanted me to pick him up
from work and we could go for a pint. I picked him up and was driving
around the corner to The Clock, in London Road, Joe picked up a pair of
pink gloves off the dashboard.
" Whose are these Eddie?" pushing the glove under my nose.
" Oh, er, er there my sisters Joe I gave her a lift yesterday"
" There Gina's" I went crimson, Joe started to laugh.
"You are alright Eddie, you can have her, she is the local bike, every
bastards rode it.
"Not my fault Joe she raped me I never stood a chance"
Joe just laughed. I have plenty of girls at the hotel. "
We had a couple more pints then went around to The Beehive I dropped
him back at the Shaftsbury Hotel, about 10p.m. He was going to meet
one of the chamber maids he said he was potty about them.
I headed back to Garston, I arrived home, put the telly on, sat down and
thought I would have a whiskey, I opened the sideboard, no whiskey,
looked everywhere, went into the kitchen, everywhere was spick and
span. I opened the bedroom door, there was Gina sitting up in bed, the
bottle of whiskey and another glass on the bedside table
" I have been waiting for you, I have had to keep myself busy with my
fingers"

" How did you get in?" "That was easy, I climbed up the drainpipe and got through the bathroom window." Her ample gorgeous breasts were resting on top of the bedclothes, she handed me a glass of whiskey, she pulled the covers back and was completely naked, she opened her legs " come on Eddie get in, right in".

I was soon stripped and in beside her, she was on fire, we kissed and caressed each other she must have had an orgasm before I arrived.

" Now lie on your back I want to ride you, it is Grand National night" she leaned over and put on a baseball cap, back to front, the one she wore at work. She straddled my erection and move back and forward, "yippee, yippee" she screamed, "Geronimo".

"That was great, Eddie, now fuck me doggy style", she got on all fours, I entered her, holding a breast in each hand, her nipples were like corks.

"Now ram it in hard, I drew back and shafted her as hard as I could, she nearly went through the wall.

" Again, again" she shouted, we came together and lay there exhausted. She poured two more whiskeys, I looked at the bottle she must have downed a good half at least.

" By the way I have moved in"

" That is good"

The landlord Phil Tongue came around for his rent the following week, he came into the back of the shop, " I will have to double your rent Eddie"

" Why is that?"

" You have someone staying with you"

"I have not", he pointed up at the line of washing, Gina`s underwear, "How long have you been wearing knickers and bras then?"

A month later I had still not found a job and I was getting pissed off, Gina was getting very possessive. "Where are you going, who with, what time will you be back, do not go out with your mates, stay in with me?"

I must have lost nearly half a stone I was getting suffocated, we went to the pictures, the Mayfair in Aigburth, she was groping me in the back row and nearly got us thrown out! The sex was great but I needed my own space.

Why do women want to take over your life and want to own you?

She started nagging if I went for a pint, after a few more weeks I told her I was leaving I did not want to settle down yet, I wanted to move on and travel a bit. That night was the first night we slept back to back. When I got up the next morning, she had left for work.

I made tea and toast and went into the lounge, on the floor near the table, I found a letter, the envelope was open. It was addressed to her friend in Manchester.

Dear Sue, I have met a smashing bloke called Eddie, we are living together and getting on swell. I have great news to tell you, I am two months pregnant. I ripped it up and put it down the toilet.

When she came home that evening, I had the tea ready, we sat at the table,

"Have you found a letter Eddie I have written to a friend, but cant find the letter, I must have dropped it somewhere, I was writing to my friend Sue to tell her I am having your baby" I kept on eating.

" Did you here me Eddie?"

" Yes I heard you and I also heard you say when we first met that you could not have any more children after your miscarriage. You have not been to the doctors, I do not believe that you are pregnant, I am sorry Gina but I am leaving tomorrow."

There was a bad atmosphere the rest of the evening, I got the whiskey out, she had a drink as well, she could drink like a fish, we were slowly getting pissed. After a few hour she got up and went into the bedroom, she came back into the lounge, naked, and stood in front of me, her legs slightly apart, holding a breast in each hand, slowly squeezing them.

" Eddie, can we have a good fuck before you go?" always willing to help out,

I dived on her. We rolled around the carpet, she was pulling my clothes off, we were both naked, having a sixty nine, it was fantastic.

"Let`s get to the bedroom Eddie for round two" she went into the bedroom and I went for a piss, she was lying on her stomach on the bed with her hands behind her back, " now Eddie, put the handcuffs on me, the are on the table"

"Where did you get them from?" "

I borrowed them off Mike the bobby when he called around for a cup of tea, you had gone out for a pint the other night Come on cuff me, you fucking pervert"

I put the cuffs on with unsteady hands, she raised her arse in the air,

" Now you dirty bastard go and get your belt and give me a good thrashing, get something to blindfold me with"

I got a scarf and my belt. "Now give me a good thrashing"

I thrashed her with the belt, she was screaming that much, that the people next door knocked on the wall, I stopped, she couched there panting, her buttocks a mass of stripes,

" Now Eddie give me a good fucking fuck hurt me"

After that I was in two minds whether to stay.
I left and she stayed in the flat. I stayed with Joe then bought a house, 62 Pemberton Road, Old Swan for £2,800 got a mortgage off the Halifax, I split the house into two, and rented out the ground floor to a young couple to pay the mortgage. I was only in the house a couple of months when a man came to the house and he said he was Mr Jones from the Noise Abatement Society and he had complaints from neighbours about people running up and down the stairs day and night possibly children.   I asked him in, showed him around. "There are no children in the house I live on my own and the couple who live downstairs have none and there out at work during the day"
"It is strange I have been her before about 2 years ago with the same complaint noises during the night"
He left looking a bit mystified.
A few weeks later I went to the Locarno Ballroom and brought a young lady back for a cup of cocoa, we were just getting to know each other better on the settee. I had just left the table lamp on to make it more romantic. We were embracing she was looking over my shoulder towards the door, all off a sudden she let out a almighty scream, she was pointing towards the door.
I looked around could not see anything, she could not get her breath, she gasped "There's a man at the door" I turned again I could see a figure of a man standing at the door it looked as though he was wearing a trilby. She was getting hysterical, she made a run for the door, I was right behind her, in fact overtook her going down the stairs.
We jumped into the car and stopped around the corner in Derby Road,
"Did you see him Eddie he had a hat on?"
"I saw something, maybe it is the drink"
"Well what are we going to do we can't sit here all night, you will have to go you will have to go back and get my handbag my flat keys are in it".
"You don't think I am going back in there do you"
"The size of you frightened of a ghost"
I drove back to the house the front door was still wide open.
"Where did you leave your bag"?
"On the chair by the door" I ran up the stairs 3 at a time, went into the lounge could not see the bag anywhere pulled the cushions up looked behind the settee, I stopped to look around the room.
Then I heard footsteps coming up the stairs, they were getting nearer and nearer I could hear them on the landing, they were outside the door. A big hand came around the edge of the door, the door was

pushed open slowly, my heart was pounding a figure walked in, and a man was standing there. It was the tenant from downstairs.

"Are you alright Eddie, I saw both doors open and thought I had better check things out." I sank back onto the armchair my heart was pounding. "Jesus Christ you nearly gave me a heart attack"

"You are as white as a sheet did I startle you?"

" Just a little, I am looking for my girl friends handbag, are there it is behind the door, I am going to run her home good night John thanks for your concern".

We went back to her flat in West Derby I slept on the settee, she said she would ring me but never did.

I went with my mate George Caldwell to the Rialto ballroom the following Saturday night we had a few pints in town then went on to the Rialto it was heaving 5 deep at the bar. All the girls dancing and the lads standing around the edge of the floor weighing up the talent. I joined the crowd at the bar, it was a good 10 minutes before I got to the front, just about to get served when this girl gets in front of me and orders her drinks.

"Do you think I am waiting for a bus, I have stood here for 15 minutes"? She said nothing just smiled, we were standing watching the dancing when I spotted the girl who got served before me she was gorgeous, long dark hair, big brown eyes great body, beautiful, she was jiving with another girl.

"Come on George let us split these two up I fancy the one in the red dress"

"Do you come her often"

"Only when it is open" she smiled

"Were do you live?" "Crosby"

"I live near you in Waterloo" I took he home to Crosby, I must have been mesmerized, I actually shook hands with her and made a date for the following Monday her name was Helen Bent.

I was really looking forward to our date, I took her to the Doric there was a few singers getting up and free sandwiches, I know how to treat a lady. Helen seemed to have mood swings some days she was all bubbly other times she would hardly talk

Helen lived with her mother and father 4 sisters and I brother her father Jasper was a bit of a character ex bosun in the Merchant Navy, he managed a betting shop; her mother worked in a television rental shop. We were both of Irish decent her grandparents called Walsh were Fenians in the 1920,s. Her beautiful dark looks coming from the Spanish

who invaded Ireland centuries before the Irish call it Black Lace.
We started to go steady, then she told me she was pregnant.
I said I would stand by her and we could get married, I loved her and
wanted to marry her pregnant or not.
About a month later she said she wanted to end the relationship and did
not want to see me again. I asked why she wanted to finish as we were
getting on so well   She said she could not explain she just wanted to call
it a day. Maybe the baby was not mine.
Sometime after I met her father Jasper, in the George pub in Crosby he
said why not call around and see Helen, I said I would think about it.
I went down a few weeks later, the baby was born the week before,
anyway we got sorted out and got married at St Helens church at Crosby
and moved in to live with her family.
The first morning of our married life Helen could not be bothered to get
up to get my breakfast. Her Mother told me Helen would never show me
any affection as she could not show her any, I should have took note.
Soon after I sold 62 Pemberton Road and bought a 4 bedroomed semi at
33 Fir Road Waterloo for £2,700,it needed modernizing and
redecorating.
Looking for work I spotted a vancanies for taxi drivers in the Liverpool
Echo in Oakfeild Road Anfield.
At the interview I was informed I would be self employed use my own
car there were no meters no radio each driver put his car keys on a
metal bar behind the front door when you got to the front it was your
turn for a fare. Which were few and far in between. A complete waste of
time. One of the drivers said he was leaving because he did not like
people telling him were to go and people talking behind his back .
I started work for Walls on the bacon and cooked meat vans, we were
based at Ensor Street, Bootle, we sold pre-packed bacon and cooked
meats to shops and supermarkets on Merseyside, each van had a driver
and a van lad. The shops or supermarket had a record card telling you
how much each shop sold each week, so you were responsible for the
amount of the order .If you put too much bacon in which had only ten
days life, what was unsold was your loss, if you put too little in, you were
in trouble if the store ran out, any bacon we took back, which was out of
date, we sold off to local cafes.
I enjoyed the job and things were running smoothly, a few months later,
I was delivering to Woolworths, Aigburth, they took a sizeable order.
We were just about to put the order on display after it had been
checked in.   When

a voice boomed out, "Just a minute I am the new manager, I will merchandise the display myself, everything has to be correct." So I left it to him. After a few days I called again, we went over to the bacon counter, there was loads of outdated bacon unsold, the manager had put the fresh bacon on top of the old bacon so the customers took the fresh bacon.

The manager came rushing over, "You will have to change all that bacon it is out of date "

"I can not change out of date bacon, it is not company policy, they have just clamped down on it"

"You will have to change it"

"Sorry, it I your fault, you have put the fresh bacon on top of the old bacon, that is why we display the bacon ourselves and are responsible for the order"

"My God, what am I going to do, I have just come over from Dublin, it is my first store, please help me, please,"

I thought he was going to burst into tears. I told the van lad, Peter, to count the packets. My next call was a local café which took outdated bacon,

Walls did spot checks to see if you had any outdated bacon on board, as the café was in the same road. I thought I would take a chance and help him. I explained to him how we sold outdated bacon to cafes,

"I can allow you 100 packets, as I will have to give the café twenty packets free" " That is great, you have saved my life, I can not thank you enough."

The following Saturday morning I was driving down Townsend Lane, I was approaching the traffic lights to turn left into Queen`s Drive, they were on green, as I turned into Queen`s Drive, a young man ran out in front of me. I swerved to my right, trying to miss him but to late.

When I stopped the van lad was hysterical, I knew I had hit him but could not see him, I got out, went around the back of the van and came around the other side, he was half under the front wheel.

There was no blood about but he was unconscious, I bent down to look closer and found that the front wheel had missed his leg and had ran up the side of his trousers.

The police and ambulance were there within minutes. A motorcycle cop came over.

" Come and sit in the van and you can make a statement, now then what happened?"

"I was coming down Townsend Lane, the lights were on green, I turned left onto Queens Drive and the man ran right out in front of me, I could not avoid him"

"No you came to the lights which were on red, you stopped and then proceeded when the lights changed to green."

"No the lights were on green and I went straight through"

"No,no you are not listening, you stopped when the lights were on red, you stopped and then proceeded to turn left onto Queens Drive."

"No the lights were on green and I went through onto Queens Drive and hit the man."

"No, no you are not listening, think carefully, you came down Townsend Lane, the lights were on red, you stopped then you turned onto Queens Drive on green, is that correct?"

The policeman was trying to help me, I did not realize at first.

"Thank you very much officer". We got out of the van, the man was standing up but they had to cut his trousers to free him. He was now standing up, a big bump on his forehead. He did not want to go into the ambulance, the motorcycle cop went over to him, he had a few questions to ask him, then he came back to me and told me the man ran across the road trying to catch the number 60 bus.

He eventually was persuaded to go in the ambulance and I heard no more about it. That was my third accident within the past twelve months.

The following Friday, I had finished my round, returned to the depot and was stocktaking on the van. I was called into the office and sacked on the spot. My area manager had called into Woolworth's at Aigburth where I had changed the outdated bacon.

The manager there had told him what a good salesman I was, helping him out of a mess. The other salesmen and myself went across the road to the Farmers Arms on Derby Road like we did every Friday.

They were quite surprised when I told them that I had got the sack.

Bob one of the other salesmen said, "That is what you get for doing people favours, they shit on you"

John Follet who was a few years older than us said that he was leaving to buy a concrete mixer and deliver ready mixed concrete to building sites. He would be under contract to Pencrete Ltd and be based Widnes. You bought the cab and chassis then rented the mixer off Pencrete.

They pay you 6/6d per cubic yard and 2 shilling per mile. The mixer held 7 yards £2=5=6d plus say ten mile round trip at 2/-per mile £1, £3=5=6d part trip, 10 trips per day £35=6=0d per day, seven days a week, £350 per week.

"Why don`t you come Eddie it is fantastic money",
"It sounds too good to be true, John"
"I have all the figures in black and white Eddie"
"How much did the wagon cost, John?"
"Only £100 deposit and £20 per week, £4400 in total on HP, about £5 a week for your mixer, too good to miss Eddie"
The only problem I had was the £100 deposit that I did not have.
" I will think about it John and get back to you next week"
I said my goodbyes to the lads and set off home. I sat there thinking the only way I could raise the deposit was by selling my car. put an advert in the Liverpool Echo and the Crosby Herald, I got about six punters, but when they saw the different coloured door they disappeared.
In the end I rang Livcock and Edwards, the local car dealers in Crosby Village, they said bring it down and we will have a look at it. I parked up outside the showroom with the passenger side right against the wall so they could not see the different shade of red.
They bought it, I came away with about £300 after the HP was settled, I lost a packet on it. John and I went for the interview at Pencrete Ltd they asked me if I had a licence I said yes, not knowing that they meant a heavy goods licence, I paid the £100 deposit, signed the contract but not the HP agreement.
John and I picked up our brand new Guy Warrior concrete mixers on the following Monday, I have never driven anything so big, 32 ton when loaded. I climbed up into the cab, it seemed we were ten feet high, then I saw the seven gears I did not know wagons had seven gears,
John drove off, I followed, grinding the gears as I went John took me to Sefton Park to practice the gears, apparently when it is loaded, you have to double your clutch and change gears every few yards, I soon got the hang of it. The next day they showed us how to operate the mixer with its four gears, we were laying kerb stones and we had to crawl along dropping the cement as we went, John asked the boss
" How do you know when the mixer is empty?"
The boss replied "When there is no more coming out"
I could not wait to get started to earn some money, but the whole thing turned out a nightmare, we did not get paid the mileage we had done but as the crow flies.
The air brakes kept failing, a small pipe used to burst under pressure and we would be off the road for days at a time. Instead of getting a full load of seven yards we would get two yards doing paths and garage bases. All the blue eyes were getting the big loads. When you went on site often

you would sink down to your axles then you would have to wait to get pulled out.

I had to drive from Waterloo to work at Widnes, the mixer only did ten miles per gallon.

The neighbours were complaining about parking the mixer and the police told me to move it. I had to park it behind The George pub and it was getting vandalized.

One morning I got a rare full load and set off to a big building site in Runcorn, as I entered the site there was a steep incline I braked to slow down.

I slowed a bit, then my foot went to the floor, no pressure, no brakes, the brake pipe had burst again, I sounded my horn frantically as I gathered speed, workmen were jumping out the way but I was still going fast.

I reached the bottom of the incline and drove into a huge pile of sand that brought me to a halt, that was it, I had had enough, left the mixer there and called it a day.

Luckily enough I had not signed the HP forms.

The next couple of months were spent getting the house into shape, my father-in-law, Jasper Bent was very good doing various jobs, especially joinery.

I was useless doing DIY, I started to decorate, I had a go at the small bedroom, thought I would get a bit of practice wall papering, I finished it in a couple of days.

I thought it looked great. I called Helen up to look at my masterpiece, she stood at the door " That is great Eddie, you have excelled yourself but it is a pity it is upside down".

Jasper was less complimentary he said it was a bloody abortion.

We installed a new bathroom and got the house rewired.

A few doors away lived a middle aged couple Mr and Mrs McRandle he loved his pint and spent most of his time in the Liver pub, one Saturday he had been drinking all day he staggered home 2 hours late for his tea and found out that his wife had given his tea to the dog, all hell broke loose he was ranting and raving.

"In that case I am going back to the pub " he went out slamming the front door behind him, Mrs McRandle opened the door and shouted "And don't come back".

He had gone about 20 yards he turned around and shouted.

"Don't forget I had you before we were married"

She shouted back" And so did all your mates"

The next night they invited us down for a drink with them in the Liver, we could hardly keep up with them, both of them knocking back double whiskers as though there was no tomorrow.

"My wives a nut case she was in town at the Pier Head bus Station She had just missed her bus, freezing cold wet through, loaded up with shopping she asked the bus conductor on the back of the bus parked nearby. "How long will the next bus to Crosby be?

"About 28for feet love" laughing loudly.

"And will it have a shithouse on the back like this one ."

After a few hours I suggested we have a game of pool this might slow them down Mrs McRandle was unsteady on her feet.

They won the toss he suggested she should break she missed the balls completely the white ball going down the pocket, she managed this 3 times she then sneezed her false teeth shot out and went down the pocket.

We had to get the pub manager over to open the table to retrieve her teeth.

"I always know when she is pissed her teeth fall out".

And a good night was had by all.

I got a job with Pepsi Cola at Long Lane, Aintree, I had to wear a uniform like an American cop, all in blue with a peaked cap and leather patches on the elbows and a big Pepsi badge on the front were called merchandisers that meant we had to put the Pepsi where the customer wanted it.

We drove a Bedford TK wagon, covered North Wales, Merseyside and Manchester,. I started off as second man, going out on different routes. We had a call at a cinema in Warrington they wanted 300 crates, we had done this delivery every fortnight for the past three months the driver, Frank went in I started to unload and stack the crates five high to truck them in. He came back after ten minutes fuming, there was a new cinema manager who decided to put the Pepsi Cola on the top floor by the protection room and the crisps etc. on the ground floor room where we usually put the Pepsi Cola so that meant us carrying the 300 crates to the top floor. Frank had told the manager he would not do it, so the manager rang our head office at Aintree.

" Your boss is on the phone, he wants to talk to you"

Frank went in and talked to the boss, the boss said he had to put the Pepsi where the customer wanted it.

Frank refused, we both got the sack, and we went back to the depot and collected our cards.

There was plenty of work about at this time you could always get a job, so I thought I would go back to butchering, I got an interview at Ben Gittens at Latimer Street off Scotland Road. He had market stalls Kirkby and St Johns market, also sold meat to various restaurants, he wanted a butcher-driver so I started on the following monday.

My first delivery was to Kirkby market, the van was an old Commer with column change, top speed 40 mph, smoke coming out of the exhaust and the gears kept jumping out, it must have been around the clock twice. I was only there a few months when the van kept breaking down so the boss Ben Gitten ordered a new van, a Bedford CF with sliding doors from G.B.E in the town centre. He had never bought a new van before.   The lads said he was a bit careful with his cash. I had to go and pick the new van up, he and his wife were coming down to Latimer Street to see it when I came back, apparently they were quite excited over the purchase, he had arranged to get a sign writer to put his name on it.   On the way back I was coming along Islington leaving the town centre, I was intending to turn left towards Latimer Street when a dog ran out, I was looking for the left turn when a car in front, a big Humber Hawk, built like a tank jammed his breaks on. I ran into the back of it, the front of the van crumbled like a tin can, the Humber Hawk, with it big bumper was not even scratched, I jumped out and asked the driver to pull around the corner in case the police came. I managed to pull some of the front wing off the front wheels.

I drove around the corner, braked the windscreen was now hanging out. I told the driver it was my fault and apologized for my carelessness. He was not bothered because his car was not damaged and did not want to take the matter any further and drove off.

I put the windscreen in the back of the van, I managed to drive off slowly, the front wheel was a bit wobbly, I turned into Latimer Street. I could see in the distance the boss and his wife standing outside the shop with some of the staff and some of the customers.

I was not looking forward to my reception, I slowly wobbled to a halt, his smile had turned into rage, he was screaming,

" You stupid bastard, drivers, I have shit better drivers, you are sacked". No sense of humour Jasper said I should have been a postman they get the sack everyday.

My next career move, I answered an ad in the Daily Telegraph from a firm an American insurance company the C.I.C.A, the Combined Insurance Company of America.

I met the team leader, Gerry O'Connor, in Bolton; he said he would make a few calls, show me how the sales went. It was personal accident insurance, written and sold off a role of policies, cold calling, business to business. He did not sell anything but I liked the idea, so he booked me in for two weeks training in London. You were paid £20 per week for the first month after the training. The training sessions were at the Seven Sisters Hotel in Tottenham London. We were shown into a large room, set out with rows of chairs set out for about forty people, the salesmen were standing around in groups some had bowler hats and brollies and were saying they were top salesmen for international companies like, Kellogg's, Imperial Tobacco and Nescafe. I felt a bit out of my depth, being a humble butcher so I kept my head down and sat on the back row.   One of the top Americans, John Drummond, was first on the rostrum,   he told us some history of the company, and it was founded by a man called Clement Stone, who through his hard work had amassed a personal fortune of sixty million pounds.

The head office was in Chicago. "Now we will get you focused, let us start with the Grand old Duke of York, Everybody sang "The Grand old Duke of York, had ten thousand men, he marched them up to the top of the hill". Everybody stood up then they sang "
He marched them down again" everybody sat down.
When it came to the part " neither up nor down" everybody jumped up and down, this went on for about five minutes, I could not believe it, apparently it is to get you alert and concentrate your mind.
We had to learn a set sales pitch, off by heart, any questions they asked you would have a good answer or rebuttal in reply e.g.
Customer have never heard of your company C.I.C.A".
Salesman "I have not heard of you but that does not say you are no good".
The American continued "If you want to be a bus driver, that is fine, if you want to raise your standard of living you have to motivate yourself nothing will come to you, you have to go and get it. You have to put your head on the line, always remember.
"A quitter never wins and a winner never quits, go one more mile"
we were getting brainwashed good style.
" Sell twenty a day, the President's way.
P.M.A, Positive Mental Attitude. Insurance, it is better to have it and not need it, than need it and not have it". After the two weeks training we were told we would sell in our own town or nearby, the policy covered you for accidents, it was very cleverly worded.

It cost £2 semi-annum and paid out £16 per week. At the end of each sales talk you had to get three yes's. You ask three questions which they will say yes to .

1. Do you drive or ride in a car? YES
2. Is it possible for you to be in an accident in the next six months? YES
3. If so could you use £16 a week? YES

When you get the three yes's you move your head up and down which infers, yes to their subconscious, then you ask them to sign up but it does not always work.   Our commission was 8/- for £2 policy, no salary. I started selling in Liverpool, it was not easy going in cold off the streets, giving a sales pitch. The first couple of weeks I averaged about thirty policies, they then organized a competition.

If you sold a hundred policies in a week, you could have a weekend in London, staying at a top hotel and attending a conference at the Hilton Hotel .At the sixth week, I sold 110 policies but I was out day and night, shops, taxies, and pubs. Helen and I had a great weekend, met all the top salesman, some of the London based salesmen had sold over 200 policies a week, they were fantastic.

But I was moved out of town to sell in Crewe,   Macclesfield and Wimslow.   I had to go bed and breakfast, there were six salesmen all together,.

   Crewe was like a ghost town, even the pubs shut in the afternoon .I was there two weeks and only sold twenty policies. Two of the salesmen went home. I was not even covering my hotel bill, the third week I only sold five policies, I had been drawing what little I had out of the bank, I thought I would stick it out until the Friday but things did not change. I could not pay my hotel bill so I would have to give them a cheque,. I went to the reception, "Could I have my bill please, I am leaving today?" he gave me the bill, it was for £84, I wrote the cheque out. The owner said," What is that for, we do not take cheques off salesmen. I have got a drawer full here, some of them are still bouncing" lonly had £18 in cash nothing in the bank.
" I will have to nip out to the bank and get some money."
He came around the counter and picked up my suitcase. "You can leave this here then."
I went and sat in a nearby café, bought a cup of tea, now what am I going to do? I must have sat for half an hour trying to think of something, I could leave my watch but it was only a cheap Newmark, not worth much, I had another cup of tea. The man on the next table left behind the Daily Mirror. I started to read it and came to the racing page.

I looked down the runners and riders and saw a horse called Orchardist which I had backed a few years back.

It was a bit old in the tooth, had poor form and was 100/6. I went to the betting shop and put £5 each way on it, said a dozen Hail Mary's and hoped it would win, if it lost I would have to do a runner ,with no petrol.

I was listening to the commentary it was a two mile race, Orchadist was not even mentioned coming to the last two furlongs, I was edging towards the door when the commentator said he had moved into fourth place. Now there were three in a line, a photo finish, Orchadist was one of them, my heart was pounding,.   I had to wait another 10 minutes until the result was announced.

Orchadist had won, I was relieved and delighted, I picked up about £110. I went back and paid my hotel bill and resigned my post, but it was a good experience, a good lesson learned from this experience, you get nowt for nowt in this life you have to work for it.

Helens mother and father moved to Southport and got a flat on the Promenade; we used to go and visit them and got to like Southport.

So we sold our house and bought a house at 21 Leicester Street between Lord Street and The Promenade, we had made £1000 profit on Fir Road we put £1000 down and borrowed £2300 off the Skipton Building Society, £3300 in total.

The house had in the past been used as a boarding house, it had eight bedrooms, it was a three storey semi-detached. My idea was to split the house into flatlets and bedsitters and live in a self contained flat on the ground floor.

The building society surveyor looked over the property, he must have had a white stick, the house had everything, dry rot, wet rot, needed re-wiring and old lead piping.

The nicest people in the world you could meet are the ones you are buying a house off until you sign up. A few months later we moved in, we had to live on the first floor until we got the ground floor ready. There was no gas on the first floor we had to leave the cooker downstairs, there was no hot water or emersion heater. We started in the kitchen on the ground floor, when we took the lino up, all it was uneven flags. Jasper and I took them all up and laid a new concrete floor. We had to boil buckets of hot water for washing etc. Jasper put kitchen units in.

I stripped all the ground floor rooms which had twelve foot ceilings, we got a local decorator in to decorate the whole ground floor,

I had borrowed £500 off the Nat West bank to cover the work, many a night we finished at midnight. After a month we had the ground floor habitable so we moved downs stairs .

Over the next few months, we split upstairs into two flatlets and two bedsits, which would bring in £16 each week, all had been furnished from the local auction rooms, also central heating was installed. The central heating boiler was located in the front cellar and it kept cutting out, it was just before midnight and the boiler cut out I went down into the cellar with lighted newspaper because there were no lights it was pitch black.

I managed to start the boiler again and started to walk back up the steps when a figure all in white came screaming out of the rear room. I nearly past out with fright I was shaking from head to foot.

My legs would not move the figure came towards me and grabbed my arm .I thought I was about to die. It was Helen covered in a white sheet I could have killed her. We advertised in the local paper, the Southport Visitor.

Our first tenant was a young girl of sixteen who was seven months pregnant by an older man, who had promised her everything, then dumped her parents did not want to know. We were not going to take any children but we felt sorry for her.

She moved into the top flat. Then the next couple were Ben and Shirley, they had a young baby, they were in there thirties, they seemed such a nice couple so they moved into the flatlet on the first floor rear.

What I did not know was that they had both been released from the Winwick Mental Hospital.

We let one bedsitter to an old soldier who had been in the army all his life he wanted to live near to the British Legion Club.

The other bedsitter we let to an elderly Irish woman, Miss Elizabeth Farrelly, from Dublin 75 years old, looked like Old Mother Riley dressed all in black. They had all paid two months in advance and things were running quite smoothly.

Then the fun started. Miss Farrelly came downstairs and knocked on our door I opened the door.

"Hello Miss Farrelly"

"Come upstairs quickly, someone has pinched a quarter of tea from my room". I followed her up into her room.

"Have you left your door open, when you went out?"

"No I always lock it"

"I can`t see anyone just taking a quarter of tea"

"Well they did and it has gone, what are you going to do about it, you had better call the police"

"I tell you what Miss Farrelly, I will give you a quarter of tea and we will keep our eyes open for anyone suspicious hanging around".

A few days later she was down again, "Come upstairs quickly, someone has been in my room".

I followed her upstairs, "Someone has pinched my knickers, they were on that chair".

Just then the front door bell rang, I went down and opened the door, two policemen stood there.

" We had a call from a Miss Farrelly, who says her room has been robbed"

"You had better come up then"

"Now Miss Farrelly what has been taken?"

"My knickers, my knickers have gone, they were blue, I have only had them a couple of years". The policemen looked at each other, then at me.   One policeman examined the door,   " The door has not been forced, did you leave it open Miss Farrelly?" " No, I always lock it"   Pointing at me she shouted "He's got them, there are some funny people about" she said glaring at me.   "We will look into it and come back to you, Miss Farrelly".

I went down to show the policeman out. When we got out onto the front step, one of the policemen said, "I think she is a bloody nutter".

"The other day she said a quarter of tea was missing".

"Well, we cannot do anything, we will leave it with you".

The following Saturday, the milkman came for his money.

"Who is that bloody old woman who comes down at 6 a.m. in the morning asking me if her kettle is on my cart, then she accuses me of stealing it"

"Oh, that is Miss Farrelly, she is a bit eccentric"

"She is bloody mad".

A few days later, I went passed her room, the door was open, she was sitting in the armchair, and there were flames three feet high coming from the fireplace.

She had the kettle on two bricks, over a tin of paraffin, "What are you doing?"

"I am boiling the kettle"

"You have a gas cooker to boil the kettle"

I do not like gas, it is dangerous"

"Well you cannot use that, you will burn the house down!" I went to the Social Services and they found her a nursing home.

I advertised her bedsitter and got another elderly lady who had been in service all her life .And had good references. When I told her she could have the room curtseyed must have thought have thought I was one of the landed gentry or she was taking the micky.

I got a job at the new Littlewoods store on Chapel Street in the butchery department, they put on a big display of meat. Five butchers started in this new store but it did not take off. They put the food department and the butchers on the first floor.

No one is going to climb stairs for food; they want to be in and out quick as they can. We were busy in the summer with the holiday trade but at the end of the season, three butchers including myself, were laid off.

It was approaching Christmas; there was plenty of work for butchers.

I got a job at Fieldens butchers, Chapel Lane, Formby, a few miles away. It was a 6 a.m. start so I had to get the 5.20a.m. Train. I did not finish until 6 p.m. it was a long week for £20.

The week before Christmas, we worked from 6a.m. through to 10 p.m. giving us some overtime. We had all the fresh turkeys to clean and pluck. On Christmas Eve the boss said, "Here Eddie, I have put £5 extra in your wages" "Thanks very much Jack".

After the first week of the New Year, I was £5 short.

"Excuse me Jack I am £5 short this week".

"That's right, that £5 you got at Christmas was only a loan to help you over the Holiday".

"Thanks Jack, happy New Year!"

Ben and Shirley kicked off on Christmas Day. This is the couple from the mental hospital   Ben came down at noon to wish us a Merry Xmas; I invited him in and gave him a large whiskey. He was only small, brown hair parted down the middle wore those thick glasses like the bottom of a milk bottle. We sat there chatting when there was a loud pounding on the door. I opened the door, there stood Shirley, dyed blond hair duffel coat and wellies with the tops turned over built like a sumo wrestler.

"Is Ben in there? "

"Yes, we are just having a Christmas drink".

With that she pushed past me. Ben stood up, he was as high as her chest.

" Hello sweet".

"You bastard, take your glasses off".

Ben obliged, She punched him smack on the chin, he went out like a light, stretched out on the carpet.

She turned and went back upstairs and came back down with a pram and suitcase, never to be seen again.

Ben managed to get back on the chair.

"She is a violent woman, met her in Winwick Mental Hospital, she won`t take her tablets, I take mine to keep me calm"

"You were in there as well?"

"Yes, that is how we met it was love at first sight."

"I can see that okay Ben, Happy Xmas".

A couple of weeks later we had just gone to bed. It was Saturday night, just after midnight. The front doorbell rang, I got up and answered it, it was an ambulance, I could see it lights flashing through the glass.

"Emergency call for 21 Leicester Street"

"Who is it for?"

"I do not know, I have not got a name".

"I do not think there I anybody up, you had better come in, I live on the ground floor so we had better go upstairs".

We went up to the top, no sign of anyone, we came down again,

"I am awfully sorry, it must be a false call".

We had just settled down again, when the doorbell rang again, the ambulance was back. "Sorry to trouble you again but this is not a 999 call, someone has called personally at the ambulance station".

Both the ambulance station and the fire station were only at the bottom of the road.

"You go and have a look yourself, there is nobody up". He went up and came down again,

"I am very sorry to trouble you again, this person has called twice at the station".

The ambulance driver turned to walk down the path when a voice shouted.

"Hang on its for me".

Ben was staggering up the road, pissed out of his head,.

"Its for me, its for me!" He was hanging on to the front gate trying to get his breath,.

"Take me to Winwick, I have got to see my psychiatrist at Winwick or I will kill myself!"

"Sorry mate, we cannot take you there, we only do emergencies, you had better ring up in the morning and make an appointment".

Ben had ordered the ambulance and could not get back quick enough, "Sorry mate, we cannot take you".

Ben jumped into the front of the ambulance and clamped his arms through the steering wheel. He would not let go. They both had him by the legs but could not drag him out.

Ben was cursing and shouting, the driver radioed the police.

Two police cars came, a black maria and two cops on motorbikes. The street was lit up like Blackpool illuminations.

Then the neighbours started to have a come out to see what was going on.

Two policemen got hold of Ben and threw him in the front garden.

Ben just lay there as they all got back into their vehicles to drive off.

Ben jumped up again and got into the back of the ambulance and hung onto the bed. Everybody got out again, finally, he was put in the cells and we got a letter from Winwick a few weeks later asking us to look after his bits and pieces until he got out and how sorry he was causing us trouble, he was a nice man who could not help being mentally ill.

A couple of months later, we were having a drink at the Cheshire Lines pub. I only had £7: two £1 notes and one £5 note. We were just finishing off our first drinks when Helen said, "Don`t look around now but Ben has jut staggered in, God is he coming over?"

"Eddie me old pal, how are you? It is my birthday today and I am as pissed as a newt can I join you?"

"Well, we were just going Ben. Here, get yourself a drink".

He took the note off me and staggered over to the bar. We made a quick exit and walked down to the Queen's on the promenade. When I got my money out, I realized that I had given him the £5 not instead of the £1, so a couple more drinks and we would have to go home.

Helen said that she would vet all the tenants in future as I took all the nutters in.

In 1969, I changed my job and went to work at Whips sausage factory at Birkdale. There were about ten people there, we boned out breasts of lamb and pig heads for sausage meat. They also made roast pork and boiled ham. I bought an old Rover P4.80 it was described in the local paper as the best Rover in Lancashire. I went to Dueadens car showroom and it was like new, a 1961 model for £275. I bought it on HP, it was two tone green, I just loved these big old Rover P4`s.

There was a butcher called Joe Poole who worked with me and he asked if I could pick him up in the morning as he only lived around the corner in Avondale Road.

The next morning I went around to call for him, I noticed a For Sale sign in the garden. As we were driving to work, I asked him about the house.

He said it had been up for sale for a year, but as it was full of tenants, nobody wanted to buy it because they were on low rents.

They were asking £5500 for it, the agent was T B Jones on Houghton Street. I called at the agents on the following Saturday morning.

"I am inquiring about the house on Avondale Road, the investment property" He handed me the details.

"Can you get a mortgage on it?"

"You cannot get mortgages on investment properties with tenants in".

Back at work, I was quizzing Joe about the house he told me that the landlady had come over from Ireland with her nephew, Michael, twenty years ago.

She told him if he maintained the house, she would leave it to him when she died but being a good Catholic, she left it to the Church, in fact, to a convent called the Poor Clares in London, so poor Michael got nothing.

I went back to the agents and asked them if the nuns would give me a private mortgage, could I have their address? .

"We cannot give out private addresses"

"You want a sale don't you?"

"Okay, but you are wasting your time".

I wrote to the Poor Clares through their solicitors, Ellis, Wood and co. in London offering £3500 and they said they would give me a private mortgage of £2500 at 11% .

I did not have a deposit so I took a second mortgage out on 21 Leicester Street with Julian Hodge from the bank of Wales using a broker called Donald Hamilton Miller from Burscough.

Joe was not too pleased having me as a work mate and also his landlord. Joe had the entire middle floor which would make two flats. He said if I could find him a smaller flat he would move out, which I did. One of the tenants died on the ground floor so I was able to let that. The top flat was empty so I split that into two. I was covering my mortgage payments but the money was going out faster on the alterations and repairs. I now had six flats in Avondale Road bringing in £48 plus £16 per week from 21 Leicester Street.

About a year later, the three brothers who lived across the road at number 18 Leicester, they were retired, and always washed their cars on the front on a Sunday. We had not seen them for a few weeks, a few days later we saw a furniture van arrive to empty the house. That night I wrote them a note to ask them if they wanted to sell and put it through their letterbox. A couple of days later, one of the brothers came over and said they were about to put the house on the market with an estate agent.

I asked how much they wanted and he said £4000. I said we were very interested and could we have a look. We went across, the house was a large semi with six bedrooms in very good condition. It had recently been rewired and there was new plumbing. I thought it was a bargain. After we had viewed we came back to the lounge, I looked over his shoulder at Helen and she nodded her head.

"I will offer you the asking price of £4000", I thought if he gets an estate agent, he would be advised to sell at a higher figure,

"You will be saving the estate agent fees as well." I added.

He accepted and we exchanged solicitors details. I always used Fletcher and Morris of Stanley Road, Bootle.

Helen asked how were we going to buy it with no money.

I explained that I would get a second mortgage on Avondale Road of £1000 and £3000 off the Halifax building society. Then we would split our flat at 21, into three flatlets and that we would pay for our new house, the one behind pays for the one in front, you could go on forever using this method as long as the houses were not too dear.

Today you would just remortgage or a buy to let mortgage

Then carry on buying but buy at the cheaper end of the market to keep down the payments. Two months later, we moved across the road, no furniture van as we just carried everything across the road ourselves.

I then started to alter and split our flat at number 21.

You were not allowed to have more than one building society mortgage or let any rooms at the time but if you don`t take chances you will get nowhere.

I was still working at the sausage factory and then working some nights well past midnight renovating. The three lettings brought in another £15 per week, that was now a total of £79 from the three houses but the money was still going out faster.

I then changed my job and went back to Littlewoods, I kept on looking for more property to buy, I noticed a big hotel on the promenade that had been empty for years.

It was called the Agincourt Hotel 47-48 Promenade must have had at least 30 bedrooms.

But I thought it would be out of my league. Most of the cheap property never comes on to the market, if someone dies and the solicitor has to sell, he will pass it on to one of his mates in the estate agent business who will pass it on to one of his mates in the property business and they will all get a cut out of it. Sometimes a solicitor will buy it himself using a limited company or nom-de-plume and make a quick killing.

I was looking in the Liverpool Echo, in the investments for sale there were two houses for Sale in Bootle, 440/442 Stanley Road, not far from where I was born.

The asking price was £5000 for the pair.

I went down and met the owner, Mr Clarke, he showed me the houses, they were huge, mid terrace and facing the North Park. There were about five tenants, all in bedsits, the sink units and meters were in but they all needed redecorating, carpeting and furnishing. I thought I would get eight bedsits in each at £5 each, a total of £80 per week. I offered him the asking price of £5000, if he would give me a private mortgage of £4000. I would offer him £1000 in cash and £4000 on the contract so he would not have to pay tax on the £1000.

I did the usual tactic, getting a £1000 second mortgage off J Hodge on our new abode and put it down on Bootle.

Now you would remortgage rather than a second mortgage the get a Buy To Let Mortgage' The vendor gave me a ten year loan of £4000.

A few months later a bought gallons of Magnolia emulsion and did the ten empty bedsits. I worked every evening, one night I awoke at 2.30a.m. I had fallen asleep on the floor.

I bought hundreds of small carpet samples to use as carpet tiles and every room had fitted carpets. It looked great when it was finished. I got the first two rooms let then used the advanced rent for the next one. A couple of months later, I had them all filled,.

I had worked hard but for the £80 per week it was worth it, so I thought. I now had an income of £159 per week! The first month was great, I collected my £80 per week. Then a few bedsits came empty, meters were broken into, furniture had gone and there was shit on the carpet. I was down to £70 per week. I cleaned the rooms out and refurbished them and re-let them. A young girl took one, she had turned up with a tiny baby, she had no where to go, her parents had been killed in a car crash.

I did not want to take children in just one room, but I felt sorry for her under the circumstances. She moved in and paid a month rent, she was on the first floor, when I called for the next months rent. She said her money had been delayed and she would pay me a soon as she could.

I went up to the top floor, then on the way down I was passing her door, which was ajar. I could hear her arguing with her friend.

"You are a right swine Terry, that landlord looked after you, no one else would take you and a baby in, you have got your money? You should have paid him".

"He is a rich landlord from Southport, it is them and us, scousers we have got nottin, nobody gives us nottin, what we have not got we take, fuck them"

As the months went by, the rents got less, the damage got worse, even the sinks were being stolen. I lived too far away to keep an eye on the property; you need the S.A.S to collect the rent in Bootle. The final straw came when the tenant on the top floor owed two months rent, he was getting his rent off the D.H.S.S. and also working in a local night club as a singer come D.J. I could not catch him in.

I spent hours sitting outside trying to catch tenants.

The D.j. rang me at 3a.m.pissed up.

"Is that you O'Brien? The fucking roofs leaking"

"Well pay your rent and I will fix it."

"It is leaking right on the fucking bed"

"Well move the fucking bed "

I was talking to the old lady who had the downstairs front room.

I asked when he came in, she said it was in the early hours about 2 a.m. but some nights he brought his amplifiers home and then left them in the hall. I asked her to phone me when he did,

I would take them until he paid the rent. The next week she rang to say that they were there, so I went down and knocked on his door. There was no answer so I took his gear. The next day, Bootle CID rang, they said I had broken into a house at 442 Stanley Road and stolen property. I explained that I owned the house and was holding the goods until I got my rent. I was told that I had to return the goods within 24 hours or I would be charged. The police drank at the club after hours where he played I took them back .

The next day the old lady rang to tell me that he had kicked her door in at 1 a.m. and had threatened to kill her for telling me about the amplifiers. His girlfriend had dragged him out; she had told him that I would be down to sort him out.

I went down the following morning but they were both out so I went again on the next morning. I opened the front door, there was blood everywhere, and it was on the wallpaper in the hallway, there was no answer when I knocked on her door so I followed the blood trail up the stairs. It led into the shared kitchen on the first floor, the sink was covered in blood, and there was blood on the stairs leading to his room. On the second floor, there were dried bloodstains on the wallpaper, I thought he must have killed her.

I found out later what had happened, an elderly couple, friends of the old lady, had come to visit her, she had told the couple about the man upstairs who was threatening her the old man went up to ask him to leave her alone. He had been expecting me to come and sort him out. so as the old man knocked on the door, he was hit on the head with a hammer he staggered down the stairs with blood gushing from the wound. He was taken to hospital and the tenant did a runner, he left Bootle altogether. The old man did recover, the good tenants could not wait to go after this episode, I was down from £80 to £30. I had another bad payer, a young women on the ground floor. I had tried for weeks to catch her in, I knocked on her door, no answer, so I opened the door,. I thought I would empty her meter. As I got in, she sat up in bed.

"Where is your rent, you are four weeks in arrears?"

She pulled the bedclothes back and sat on the edge of the bed, she only had a tea shirt on, huge boobs hanging down to her navel her legs apart it looked like the Mersey Tunnel

"I have lost my job and have no money. You can fuck me if you want, that is the only way I can pay"

"Sorry love, but I cannot spend pussy".

When I got home, I rang Mr Clarke who I had bought the houses from. I told him I was too far away to look after the houses properly. I asked if he would take them back and he could keep the £1000 deposit and the payments I had made. He agreed, thank God. In future.

I would stick to properties in Southport, all that work and hassle in Bootle for nothing!

Our next door neighbours from number 16 Leicester St, Jack and Freda, two Cockneys, used to come in for a drink or a chat but they never knew when to leave. Once or twice Helen and I had fallen asleep and they would wake us up after midnight to say they were going. They called around to say they were returning to London and would I be interested in their house.

I got another mortgage off the Abbey National and bought it, then number 12 came on the market so I got a mortgage off Northern Rock building society, so now I had a third mortgage on 18 for the deposit 16, a second mortgage on 16 for the deposit on 12, I now had 12, 16, 18 Leicester Street. If I could buy number 14 it would make a good development site for flats or a cul-de-sac for houses. By 1970, I had stopped working as a butcher and did the houses full time. My rental income was about £160 per week; I had five mortgages and four second mortgages to pay so I was not making a fortune but a good wage. During the 60s and early 70s the property market was booming, house prices doubled within a matter of months in the South.

I went to see my solicitor, Mr Edgar Morris of Fletcher and Morris at Bootle I mentioned the big hotel on Southport Promenade, which had been empty for years. He said, " Do you mean the Agincourt Hotel facing the Floral Hall?"

"That is right, I was wondering how much it would be".

"I do not know Eddie but a Mr Silverton used to own it, he is Jewish like myself. I know he has another property in Cemetery Road which are flats, you may be able to ask someone there for his address".

I went around to Cemetary Road but none of the tenants would give me the address of the owner. I kept on trying, hanging about hoping someone would help me, remember, a quitter never wins and a winner never quits. A week later I was passing and I spotted a man repairing the roof. I turned around and went back and I asked the man who the owners were. He gave me the owner's name and phone number in London. I called the owner, Mr Richard Sherrington, he said he was just about to put it on the market. He was looking for offers over £22,000. told him I was interested, he came up the week after to show me around. He came at lunchtime I offered him £22,500 On the 14th of December1972.It had been completely stripped out, it had four bay windows with two entrances in between, it had 24 bedrooms, I offered him £22,500 and he accepted it. I thought it was a bargain, the only problem was, I did not have the money.

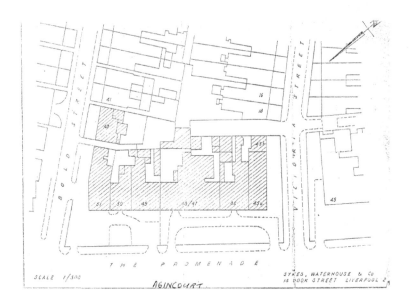

No problem were there is a will there were is a way. I knew there was equity in my other properties but to get a commercial loan they would want 1/3rd deposit which I did not have. My cousin, Chris Larkin, who was an insurance broker he worked for Target Life and had connections with Slater Walker, a merchant bank run by whizz kid Jim Slater and M.P. Peter Walker. We put the proposition to them to purchase the Agincourt Hotel, split it into 14 self-contained flats. There was a government grant available of about £3000 per flat, total grant £42000. Which would well cover the cost of conversion. I got an architect Brian Marsden to draw up some plans and applied for the grants, he was, recommended by Peter Butterfield of Rimmers Estate Agents. All these professional men have Rotary Club or Freemason membership, they know who is ideal for your job, they all piss in the same pot and look after each other before you.

Chris Larkin put the proposition to Slater Walker and we were waiting for a reply. I mentioned the project to my local insurance broker, Tim

Woods of the Southport Insurance Company. He said he knew a finance bank called First National Finance Corporation in London they were lending millions of pound to anyone. I sent the site plan, plans of the conversions and projections to them About a week later, Tim Woods rang up to say that they wanted to meet us in their Manchester Office. We met a Mr Michael Hanman and a Mr John Hall, both young men in there thirties, you always expect bank managers to be much older. I went through the proposition, I needed £22500 to purchase the Agincourt Hotel, convert it into 14 self-contained flats with aid of a council grant of £3000 per flat, a total of £42000 which would cover the cost of the conversions, then rent them out.

Mr Hanman then asked me what I had done in the past. I told him that after leaving school at 15, I worked as a butcher, then about five years ago I started to buy houses and turn them into lettings. I had five properties and a rental income of about £200 per week.

I had no account available I did not even have an accountant.

"What would you like to do in the future, would you continue as a landlord or would you go into being a developer?"

"I would like to develop later on".

He put the site plan on the table, "This site has great potential Mr O`Brien my colleagues and I have worked out a scheme for a purpose built block of 72 flats on stilts with penthouses on top and car parking underneath. It is an ideal site, one acre of land overlooking the sea.

In the present property boom, they would sell like hot cakes, what do you think? How much would you say it would cost to build a block like that?"

Being a butcher, I did not have a clue, "I would say about one million pounds."

"Well, you are not far out at all. Would you like to have a go at it, go on fill your boots?"

Without any hesitation, I said, "Yes, alright, I will have a go", must be the mad Irish side of me.

"Right, we will drink to that". John Hall opened the cocktail cabinet, "What will you have?" "A bottle of beer please" The other all had gin and tonic.

"Go back and buy the rest of the block, plus the Hotel on the side, 43 Bold Street.

We will give you 90% of the purchase price and 100% of the developing cost at 7% over the base rate."

I did not even know what the base rate was.

"We will take a first charge on the promenade properties, and a second charge on your other properties"

On the way back to Southport, Tim Wood said he could not believe my luck, "You have no accounts, you ask to borrow £22500 and they offer you an open cheque over a million pounds."

My lucky day I thought or was it He explained that First National Finance Corporation was not a traditional bank, not in the old school tie brigade. It was started by a man called Pat Mathews whose father had been a barrow boy and they were lending millions of pounds to all and sundry on the strength of the booming property prices.

The next day I got a letter off Slater Walker offering me an advance of £50,000 to do the hotel conversion, signed by Mr J A Bertenshaw, it was just for 47/48 The Promenade, just 14 flats conversion. I rang Chris Larkin to tell him I had been to F.N.F.C and that they wanted me to do the whole block, demolish it and build a purpose built block of 72 flats and they had offered me an open cheque He said to keep the offer running with Slater Walker, they might lend more finance at a cheaper rate. On the 17th of January, 1973, I got a letter from both banks saying that they were both coming to see me at home, Slater Walker at 12pm and F.N.F.C. at 1pm, I supposed they wanted to see my home environment. Chris Larkin and Mr Bertenshaw arrived spot on 12 noon. I took them into the living room, my pet rabbit, Lucifer, was sitting on the armchair,   "Sorry Mr Bertenhaw, I will just put the rabbit out", not a very good start. Helen brought coffee in and then we got down to business. We discussed the project, pension plans, insurance but they would not lend any more than the £50000. At 18% the interest rates were practically the same.   The front doorbell went and Helen answered it, it was F.N,F.C Mr Hanman and Mr Hall, the hour had gone like two minutes. Helen came in and told me there was someone to see me, "Excuse me please",

I went into the front room, shook hands and said to Mr Hanman.

."Is everything in order as agreed?"

"Yes, I have the offer here in my brief case"

"Good, because I have Slater Walker in the back room and they have offered me a facility" "You will be alright with us, they are a Mickey Mouse outfit".

I read the offer and it was agreed. I went to tell Slater Walker I would be taking the F.N.F.C money, Chris was very disappointed a he had worked hard to get the offer, but I felt that the F.N.F.C advance gave me more scope.

I needed the 10% deposits for the hotels so I asked my brothers George and Allan if they would like to invest any money in the project. If they would invest £15000 between them, I would give them the properties in Leicester Street and Avondale Road. What was owed on them was less than half of what they were worth. I could not give them now as I needed the income because F.N.F.C wanted to take a second charge on them. I could buy the whole block and get planning for the 72 flats, the site would be worth a fortune. They both agreed to invest. I completed the purchase of 47/48 the Promenade on the 24th of July, 1973.

Now I had to find out who owned that other hotel. Number 46 was full of students, one of them told us that a Ron Ellis, a local DJ and entrepreneur owned it and that he was at the Toad Hall night club most evenings as DJ. So that night, I went down to Toad Hall and waited until he came off stage. He headed straight for the gents, so I followed him in, "Are you Ron Ellis?" He took about three steps back, must have thought I was going to hit him.

"Who are you?"

"I am Eddie O`Brien. I want to buy 46 the Promenade off you".

"How much are you offering"?

How much do you want?" "£20,000"

"Too much I will give you £15000"

"Make it £16000" "Done". We shook hands, " That is with vacant possession."

" Agreed"

The next one, 45a, was in three flats and had just been sold at auction by Hatch and Fieldings estate agents of Lord Street to their own sales room porter, a Mr Lloyd, the hammer went down very fast when he made a bid of £8000, I offered him £11000 and he accepted. I then called at number 49, the owner Mr Rimmer, lived on the ground floor, an elderly gentleman, in his late seventies. He showed me around the rooms all in bedsitters, mainly older women, they were large rooms with sixteen feet high ceilings, no hot water in the rooms or in the bathrooms. The only heating they had was one bar electric fires.

How the old people survived in the winter, God only knows, you could smell the damp. We went back down to his flat, he said he wanted to sell but to stay and live there.

"That is not possible I need vacant possession before I can buy, you cannot have the money and keep the property".

I was there about an hour, he told me his life story and showed me his coin collection, he seemed a nice old man and I said I would call and see him again.

A few days later, I called at number 50, the owners did not live there, one of the tenants, a Mrs Marshall gave me the name and address of the owners who lived in Blackpool, a Miss Crystal and Miss Kaye. I wrote to them asking would they consider selling number 50.

They wrote back and said they would come over and show me around the property as they were thinking of putting it on the market. agreed a figure of £16.500 with the tenants in, twelve all together, they wanted double that with vacant possession, it was in the same condition as next door, the sale went ahead, two properties to go, 51 the Promenade and the adjoining property, 43 Bold Street around the corner.

I was getting very excited now kidding myself I was a Property Tycoon but it was all O.P.M. Other Peoples Money the secret of the property business.

I went to 43 Bold Street it was a doss house, the owner did not live there but had a manager there called Roy, he showed me around. It was full of down and outs and alcoholics, we entered the dinning room, they were having lunch, about twelve men The Manager came in, he had a loaf of sliced bread balanced on one hand against his chest.

Who wants bread?" he shouted. Some of the men raised their hands, he threw the bread across the room like playing cards and the men would leap up and catch it.

I eventually bought it for £12,000. I went back to see Mr Rimmer at number 49,a week later about 12 noon.

"Come on Eddie, I will take you out to lunch over at the Floral Hall,"
We had a nice lunch and sat there talking trying to strike a deal.
"Those plants look dry Eddie". He picked up the water jug off the table
and preceded to water the various plants, they were all plastic.
He called the waiter over for the bill, when he got the bill he handed it to
me and said he had forgotten to bring his wallet, this man is not as daft
as he looks, I thought, eventually I got the property for £18,000, with the
tenants in. The last property was number 51 the Bonds Hotel, the
smallest hotel on the block, I knocked on the door, the owner Mr
Shepherd answered the door .
"Come in, I have been waiting or you," we went into the front lounge.
He was a about 50 years of age, slight build horn rimmed glasses on and
his hair parted in the middle " I see you have bought the rest of the
block"   "
Do you want to sell?"
"I certainly do"
" How much do you want?"
"£60,000"
I laughed. " £60,000 you only paid £7,750 for it last year"
" It does not matter what I paid for it, I have got you by the balls,
without me you cannot get planning for a new block, so there".
"I will offer you £30,000, four times what you paid for it".
" It is £60,000 or nothing".
"It is nothing I have only paid £96,500 for the rest of the block"
"You will be back" he said as I departed.
I rang Hanman at FNFC, he said to leave it for a few weeks and then go
back, he also said if there were any other potential sites on the
Promenade to go and get them, as money was in abundance.
I kept going back to number 51 and after a few months got him down to
£40,000, I got in touch with Hanman, he said to go ahead, I exchanged
contracts putting £4,000 down, so the whole site cost £136000, seven
hotels all together, on a one acre freehold site.
I saw another property number 10 The Promenade which was in a block
of three, numbers 10, 11 and 12, the asking price was £17,750 it was a
former rest home which had closed down. I arranged to view with estate
agent Edward Jackson, I offered £14750 which was accepted and asked
for a contract. I rang Hanman at FNFC, he said to go ahead and get the
other two adjoining properties. My architect Brian Marsden obtained
planning permission on 10, 11 and 12 the Promenade for a flat
development. I have exchanged contracts on number 10 the

Promenade.

Seeing that things were going so well I looked at a large detached house at 17 Westbourne Road Birkdale not far from the Royal Birkdale Golf Course it was split into two flats with the ground floor vacant. We could sell our house at 18 Leicester Street and move there. The asking price was £17,500, we went to view and offered £15,500 which was accepted. I would have to get a second mortgage on 18 Leicester Street for£3,000 to put down on Westbourne and then sell number 18. We put £3000 down on 17 Westbourne and because it had a tenant in we couldn`t get a building society mortgage, so we borrowed £12,500 off Slater Walker, which is more of a finance bank.

We had the ground floor and the basement which was once the snooker room.   I managed to move all the tenants from the hotels 49 and 50 without upsetting any of them, moving some of them into my own flats or other suitable accommodation.

The last two to leave number 49 were two sisters, Mable and Mary, they were In their late seventies, they had not been out of the flat which was on the top floor for years because they could not get back up the stairs. They were going to move to the ground floor at 21 Leicester Street and they were delighted. We put all their furniture in my van and one of the sisters, Mable asked if I could stop at the local general shop and get a loaf, six egg and a quarter of tea.

" I am supposed to be a budding tycoon, not doing your shopping."

They laughed I went into the shop and got what they wanted, I was about to drive off when Mary said we would have to go back to the Promenade as she had left her teeth in the flat, we went back to the Promenade.

" I will get them for you Mary".

" They are in a cup on the mantelpiece Mr O`Brien ".

They soon settled in and were happy. Then disaster struck, Mr Morris my solicitor rang up to say the bank F.N.F.C had gone bust or insolvent, the big property bubble had burst.

" How will that affect me?"

" Well you will not be able to complete the purchase of 10 and 51 the Promenade and if you don't complete they could make you bankrupt, you could lose everything including your house."

At this time bank and finance companies had lent millions of pounds on property on building land and got their fingers burnt when the property market crashed and the collateral was down valued. All the big developers were limited companies they could go into liquidation and walk away owing nothing, but I was in partnership with Helen and was personally responsible for my debts. Before buying all this property I asked my new accountant, Colin Mead should I form a limited company, he said leave it for now and see how it goes.

My solicitor suggested I go and see Mr Sheppard at 51 the Promenade.

" Come in Eddie" We were on first names now seeing he was going to make such a big profit. " Would you like a coffee?" he shouted to his wife, Shirley

"Eddie's here, could you make us a coffee?"

" I have got a bit of a problem Jeff, my solicitor applied to the bank F.N.F.C for the £36,000 to complete your sale and the bank have written back to say they have gone insolvent."

" How do you mean?"

"They have gone bust."

"Banks don't go bust bankrupt"

"This one has"

His wife Shirley jumped up screaming, " When do we get our money, you promised us £40000 and we want it now, don't try and con me, you have bought half the Promenade, now you say you have no money".

He chipped in, " And four houses in Leicester Street don't try and kid me"   He got on his feet, he was dancing with rage, she was holding her head in her hands.

"Oh God, oh God, I will get a bucket of stones and break all your windows."

" The best thing I can offer you, seeing that you only paid £7,750 for this place last year, you can keep the £4,000 deposit I have given you and we will call it a draw."

He said," you can stick your £4,000, we want £40,000 and we are going to get it. If you don't we will make you bankrupt, in fact I will ring my solicitor now, you stay there you Bastard."

" Get him Jeff, get him, we will make you regret this you bastard."

"It is not my fault the banks gone bust, you have made £4000, lost nothing, if you make me bankrupt you will get nothing, it is all borrowed money".

" No, but we will have the pleasure of seeing you go down",
she definitely had the Liverpool chip. He got through to his solicitors, Russell and Sutton, had a brief conversation, then put the phone down.

" Right, you have 28 days to come up with the money or we will make you bankrupt and that is a promise"

They started arguing, "We have been married 33 years and you have put me through this you bastard", she screamed. I made a quick exit.
Helen was calm but I could see the shock in her face. " What are we going to do now Eddie?"
" I don't know love, I just don't know. I had not told her we were in the same position on number 10 the Promenade.
I sat down and mad a list of the properties made a list of properties and what we owed on them:

21 Leicester street first charge Skipton B/S		£2,300
second charge Julian Hodge		£1,000
12Leicester street first charge Northern Rock B/S		£8,000
Second charge Julian Hodge		£1000
16 Leister street first charge Abbey National B/S		£9,000
Second charge Julian Hodge		£2,000
18 Leicester street first charge Halifax B/S		£3,000
Second charge Julian Hodge		£1,000
Avondale road Poor Clares nuns		£2,500
Second charge Julian Hodge		£,1000
Promenade 45 46 47 48 49 5O		£96,500
10 promenade	Vendor	£13,275
51 promenade	Vendor	£36,000
Midland bank	overdraft	£10,000
Natwest bank	overdaft	£5,000
	Total	£191,575

Bit of a mess, I thought, I had better unload some properties, I found a buyer for number 10
the promenade at £16,750, making £2,000 profit, a Mr Norman Ibbotson was the buyer, he was in the central heating business.

FIRST NATIONAL FINANCE CORPORATION LiMITED
BANKERS

P.O. BOX 505
FIRST NATIONAL HOUSE
FINSBURY PAVEMENT
LONDON EC2P 2HJ

01-638 2855
TELEX 887518
CABLES FIRNAT LONDON EC2

REGISTERED OFFICE FIRST NATIONAL HOUSE FINSBURY PAVEMENT LONDON EC2P 2HJ   REGISTERED NUMBER 59814 ENGLAND

Our ref: MJH/GJH/C.15404   24th May 1974

E. O'Brien Esq.,
615 Lord Street,
Southport,
Lancashire.
PR9 0AN

Dear Mr. O'Brien,

I am writing with reference to your visit to this office
last month and our discussions concerning your site on
the Promenade at Southport.

I write to advise you that as I promised I once again put
your file to my Board with a request that we withhold taking
precipitous action against you for two months, in consideration
for which we would receive a fee of £10,000 and interest at 7%
over Base Rate on your outstanding balances.

I also requested that for a further fee of £4,000 we advance
to you a further £40,000 to enable you to complete the purchase
of the property known as 51 The Promenade. Unfortunately, they
have not acceded to this request as our chief surveyor upon
re-appraising the site was of the opinion that it would not be
to our best interest to put out any further monies.

I am sure you will appreciate our thinking and you can at least
be certain that you have a further two months in which to arrange
the sale of your site and during that time I will allow interest
to accrue.

No doubt you will keep me closely advised as to what arrangements
you are making with the vendor of number 51 The Promendde and as
to how you are progressing with the sale of the whole area.

85

A. Dean M.C.B.A.   *D. Dean* M.C.B.A.

Officers to the Sheriff of Lancashire, Merseyside and Cheshire
CERTIFIED DISTRAINT OFFICERS AUCTIONEERS and VALUERS

E. O'Brien,
t/a Shore Building Contractors,
17 Westbourne Road,
Southport.

Office Nos 5-6,
HOPE CHAMBERS,
7 LEATHER LANE,
DALE STREET,
LIVERPOOL,
L2 2AF
Tel: 051-236 4751 - 051-236 6406

17th August, 1976

Dear Sir,

Re: Swiftbrook Construction Ltd. -v- E. O'Brien t/a

With reference to my recent letter a further warrant of execution has now been issued for which I enclose the official notification of the amount due.

As there are four warrants of execution outstanding against you, I would be pleased if you would give this matter your most immediate and personal attention, as with so many warrant against you any one of these plaintiffs can proceed to bankruptsy.

Yours faithfully,

He opened it up as a rest home, one of the many he would open in future , to this day, he says I ripped him off on that property, not that I put him on his feet as the was the case, that was one headache less.

Mr Hanman from FNFC wanted a meeting with my solicitor Mr Morris to discuss the Promenade site, I was now falling behind on the interest payments. I was trying to pay other loans and mortgages and keep everybody happy, we met at Mr Morris` office at Stanley Road Bootle, Mr Hanman, who had just driven up from London, was accompanied by a Mr Chris Bell who was a tall thin man wearing glasses, in his thirties, a right bastard.

Mr Morris` offices had threadbare worn carpets, all the walls painted brown and green, being Jewish it had not been decorated for years.

Mr Hanman wanted to know what propositions we had to rectify the situation, We talked for over an hour but no solutions.

Mr Hanman said he had had no alternative but to call in the loan and make me bankrupt.

Chris Bell was leaning back on his chair with both feet on Mr Morris` desk. " Go on Mike, go for him, cut his legs off, make him bankrupt" He thought it was a huge joke. What was annoying them was that they had travelled up from London and had not been offered a cup of coffee or washroom facilities which was standard practice.

Mr Morris said that "It was First Nationals fault, they had gone bankrupt, creating the situation we find ourselves in".

Mr Hanman said, " Mr O`Brien has changed the format from converting the flats to a new development".

I had not spoke up until now, "No, it was you who changed the format I asked you asked you to lend me £22,500 to convert one hotel into 14 flats; it was you who offered me an open cheque to buy the whole site and it is you who has gone bankrupt, causing this problem."

Hanman said, "You are out of your depth, you are a cowboy"

"Well I am in a cowboy bank, where is your horse?"

That did not go down well at all.

Chris Bell said, " Come on Mike sort him out, go for him".

Hanman said, " You will be hearing from the Banks solicitors who will make you Bankrupt" and they departed.

A month later I got the bankruptcy writ from Sheppards at 51 the Promenade. I took it down to my solicitor, Mr Morris, he was sitting behind his desk "Will you look after this for me Mr Morris please?"

"What is it?"

" It is a bankruptcy writ from Sheppards at 51 the Promenade".

I put it on his desk, he did not even look at it, he pushed it back to me
" No I cannot"
"How do you mean you cannot?"
"Well you have no money left have you? my boy"
"But I have just done £200,000 worth of business with you, this past year".
" But that is all water under the bridge my boy, good day" typical Jewish reaction.
I rang other solicitors but nobody wanted to know, I tried to get legal aid but they said we do not give legal aid to speculators, it looks a though we would have to go to the High Court in Liverpool on our own.
We arrived at Court at 10a.m. the following Monday, the Judge was a Mr Morris Jones, QC who sat upon his throne; we were at floor level looking up. The Sheppards did not have the guts to come themselves they had a barrister and solicitor Rusell and Sutton.
Their barrister kicked off, " We are here today to obtain specific performance against E and H O`Brien, they entered into a contract to purchase my client`s Hotel, Mr and Mrs Sheppard at a price of £40000, they have failed to complete the purchase and owe my Client £36000, plus interest and all legal costs."
He went on for an hour quoting section this and section that, a load of legal jargon we could not quite understand, he then sat down.
" Now Mr O`Brien, what have you got to say in your defence?"
Judge Morris Jones said straightening his wig,
"Well your Honour, I would like an adjournment"
"Why is that Mr O`Brien?"
"Well your Honour, they have a barrister and a solicitor, we have no one to look after our legal interests."
"Why are you not legally represented then, Mr O`Brien?"
"We have no money"
" Well you won`t get any then, will you? Carry on".
" How can I carry on, if I cannot understand the legal jargon? What is Specific Performance? How can I answer questions I don`t understand
The Judge leaned forward and raised his voice,
" Specific Performance means you owe Mr and Mrs Sheppard £36000 after exchanging contracts and you must pay it"
"I have not got it"
"The Law says you must pay it"
"I have not got it"
"This Court says you must pay it"

"I have not got it"

"Well you must pay it"

" I have not got it.

 The judge was getting annoyed

"You cannot get blood out of a stone, My bank First National Finance Corporation have gone bankrupt, I have told them to keep the £4000 deposit as they only paid £7750 for the property a year before, so they have lost nothing and made a profit".

Their barrister jumped in, "It does not matter what they paid for the property, it I what you owe, £36,000 plus costs legal fees loss of business revenue and interest

It went on all day until 3 p.m., the Judge retired to his chambers, came out about half an hour later,

"Well Mr O`Brien, what have you got to say, before the verdict?"

"I am being steam rolled through here, I do not think it right ".

"Rubbish, I find in favour of Mr and Mrs Sheppard, you must pay £36000 plus Court Costs, Legal fees and interest within 28 days, or you will be made bankrupt".

"Thank you very much, your Honour".

I found a buyer for 18 Leicester Street, a Mr Saica, an Italian who wanted to open a restaurant on the ground floor, I needed a quick sale, we agreed £12750. But before I could complete the sale I found out the Halifax Building Society had applied for repossession on the following Monday, at Southport County Court, I got to the Court at 10am, we were first on. I explained to the court that I had a buyer for the house and they house had been surveyed and we were just waiting for the mortgage offer. Mr Saica the buyer had already a mortgage offer on another property, which he hadn`t bought. I asked for extra time to sell but the Court refused .

The Recorder said "Mr O`Brien you have appeared before this County Court over 100 times and we are getting fed up with you I am refusing to give you extra time".

The Halifax Building Society gave the house to Hatch and Fieldings estate agents to sell. I had to hand the keys over but kept a spare set.

I was so near the sale completion. The Nat West Bank with court action was now threatening me, and I only needed a week or two for the sale to go through. I decided to change the Yale lock on the front door and bolt the backdoor, so if they brought a viewer round they could not get in to view, which would delay matters.

I asked my tenant across the road at 21 Leicester Street if they saw any viewers to ring me, but it was a selling agent who rang me up and said they had taken the viewer round and could not get in.

Had I give them the right keys. I said I had and they must have got them mixed up, they decided to change the lock.

My tenant at 21 rang me the next day to say they had changed the front door lock. I went that afternoon, climbed in through the kitchen window, which I had left slightly open and changed the lock again.

The week after, my tenant at 21 rang to say there had been another viewer there and they could not get in.

A few days later they changed the lock again. I went back and changed the lock again.

The next day Mr Saica got his mortgage through and we completed the sale the next week, I did my own search at the Town Hall to speed things up. I paid £4000 to Nat West to pay off the first mortgage. F.N.F.C had now put charges on all my other properties except my house at 17 Westbourne Road.

Things were looking a bit bleak.

The Nothern Rock issued a Writ foe repossession on 12 Leicester street, and the Abbey Nation on 16 Leicester street

Time running on fast on the bankruptcy. I was sitting there scheming, I got out the Yellow Pages and looked up all the breweries in the area, to see if they wanted a site for a hotel or pub development on Southport promenade.

About four or five were interested, they were Boddingtons, Higsons, Whitbreads and Bass Charrington.

Owen Oysten had opened an estate agent in Southport, I rang him and told him I was thinking of putting the site on the market.

He said he would come around and advise me, I met him on the Promenade, he looked around the properties, he was a tall man with long blonde hair and a short goatee beard and a large brimmed hat, he looked like Buffalo Bill.

We were standing on the top floor overlooking the bay out to Blackpool, you could see the Tower in the distance .

" I would be looking at offers over £330,000 for a prime site like this, it will never come again, you have done marvellously well, getting it together"

"I will think about it, thanks for coming". I was very surprised at his valuation, I did not think it was worth anywhere near that much, now I know how much to ask the breweries. Boddingtons and Higsons lost interest when I told them the price but Bass Charrington and Whitbreads were very keen, both offered the asking price, £330,000. I contacted my new solicitor Jack Coulthurst of Davis Campbell and co Liverpool and they sent a contract out to both Bass Charrington and Whitbreads, first one to exchange contracts got the site.

I had only five days left before I went bankrupt I asked my solicitor to write me a letter saying that the breweries had been sent a contract for the Agincourt site so I could show Mr and Mrs Sheppard. When I received the letter the following morning I immediately went down to Sheppards at 51 the Promenade, Mr Sheppard answered the door, in a harsh tone he said, "What do you want?"

" I have got good news, I have a letter here that confirms two breweries want to buy the site at £330,000, if you give me time to sell and withdraw the bankruptcy I will be able to pay you £36,000, I will pay all the legal costs and the interest".

I showed him the letter, he read it,

"Come in, Here sit down Eddie, make him a cup of coffee Shirley, I will get on the phone now to my solicitor and withdraw the bankruptcy" which he did. His wife brought the coffee in,

"You know Eddie I would not have made you bankrupt at the end of the day were both Scousers, we are both working class family men, you caught us on a bad day, didn't he, Shirley?"

"Yes it was just one of our off days, wasn`t it Jeff?"

"You know Eddie, I take my hat off to you, not many would have taken this on you have a lot of guts"

"I am glad it is sorted out now Jeff now we will all be happy, I will get my solicitor to write to yours, I am off now Jeff cheerio."

"You are welcome here any time Eddie, if you want to pop in for a cup of tea" lovely couple. Not only were we clearing all our debts we would come out with £150,000 I could not believe it. I rang Hanman at F.N.F.C and told him the good news he said he would not take any action against us and would send us a final settlement figure.

I decided to take Helen out for an Indian meal at Mr Barrys on Lord Street to celebrate our good fortune, we were so happy.

Whitbreads were dragging their feet on the sale but Bass Charrington were forging ahead with the paperwork. Unfortunately, the joy was short lived. Six weeks later Bass Charrington sent the contract back unsigned as they had discovered in the last few weeks the Town Hall had made the Agincourt a listed building and put a preservation order on it so the brewery could not demolish it, the breweries pulled out all together. Who rings up the next day, Jeff Sheppard. "How is it going

Eddie?"   "Well Jeff there is been a slight hiccup, I had better come down and see you" I pulled outside the Sheppards, I looked up to the roof, and I had asked a roofer known as Tricky Ricky to secure some chimney pots on Sheppards chimney to keep him sweet

"I have nearly finished now Eddie, just a few bricks to put back"

"Thanks Ricky"

Mr Sheppard opened the door, his face full of apprehension.

Mrs Sheppard was standing by the fire place, she had just come back from the hairdressers, she flicked her ash into the fireplace,

"Now don`t give us any bad news, we can`t take anymore"

" Well I am afraid it is bad news, the council have made the block a listed building and it cannot be pulled down so the brewery have withdrawn from the sale"

She started screaming abuse he went bananas, jumping two foot in the air, "You bastard, you bastard you fucking bastard I will fix you"

"I am sorry but it is not my fault they have made it a listed building or that the banks gone bust"

" You just stand there, I will get on to my solicitor and make you bankrupt double quick" he got through but could hardly speak with rage,

"Make him bankrupt straight away do him, do him You bastard you will rot in Hell" she screamed .

She was leaning against the fireplace looking into the fire, her head on the mantlepiece. The next thing I heard was a rumble of bricks coming down the chimney, then a huge fall of soot, she was covered head to foot, she looked like one of the black and white minstrels, I could not help but laugh, it was an instant reaction.

They were not amused, "Get out, get out" they screamed.

The only good thing was that it would take them months to get a new court date.

A few days later I got a letter from Hanman F.N.F.C wanting to know how the sale was progressing and would I ring him. I rang him and told him what happened. He was not too pleased and he would charge me a £10,000 penalty fee that would give me a further two months to sort things out so now instead of £96500 I owe £106500 plus all the interest which was now rolling up so I was now paying interest on the interest. Hanman told me to sell the 4 houses I had in flats and F.N.F.C. would take the profit from the sales. They were 12,16,21 Leicester Street and the house in Avondale Road, that meant I would lose the rents the only income I had.

He wanted them valued by a estate agent, I asked Andy Coburn of

Entwistles to value them as low as possible as they had sitting tenants on low rents. I sent the valuation down to Hanman it was £35,000 it would give them £9,000 profit. Hanman said get them on the market. My plan was to sell the 4 houses to my father in law Jasper on paper then sell 12 and 16 Leicester Street with vacant possession for £35,000 this would pay for the 4 properties giving me 21 Leicester and Avondale Road free. I had to move some tenants about but after a few months I sold 12 Leicester Street to a plumber Jack Priestly for £17,500 he turned it into a guesthouse and 16 to another plumber Neil Weatherby who did the same.

I then planned to convert the other 2 properties into flats. About two months later Chris Bell rang up from F.N.F.C. he was the nasty one who came up with Hanman who was telling Hanman to make me bankrupt, he said he was coming up to their Manchester office and wanted to look at the site on The Promenade as they had a potential buyer.

Also he wanted to look at the 4 properties I had sold for £35,000 as he thought they were undervalued and sold to cheap. I had got Avondale Road vacant and had put up scaffold up at the front he would be expecting it to be full of tenants. I used to sit for hours praying and scheming for answers, desperate days desperate measures.

I would change the road signs, swap Avondale Road with Knowsley Road Sign show him the same number in Knowsley ,it would only be for 20 minutes .

I He arrived on the following Monday at 2 p.m. my mates had swapped the road signs just at one end and were standing by to replace them as soon as he was gone before some one rang the council.

He had a quick look around the Agincourt site took a few photos then said he was running late

"Mr O`Brien I have just about got time to look at those other properties are they far away?

I had his car blocked in.

"No Mr Bell we will go in my car as I know where they are."

I thought I would go to "Avondale Road" first so they could get the road signs back as soon as possible.

"Be as quick as you can I have to get back to London".

After "Avondale Rd" I turned around in the road and went back the same way then along the Promenade and stopped outside 21 Leicester Street he could see 12 and 16 across the road.

"They seem big houses for £9,000 each Mr OBrien"

" Do not forget Mr Bell they have sitting tenants with low rents and there is a property slump on at the moment, If you were in London or the South it would be a different story, I was lucky to get rid of them."

"O,K, I seen enough I will have to dash "

I never heard anymore about them it had worked a treat, thank God.

A couple of weeks later I was having a drink in the Marine Bar on the Promenade I was on the way out to the gents when a small elderly gentleman bumped into me, " I am frightfully sorry old boy" he said in a posh accent.

"Do forgive me, well I never, how are you?"

"I am fine thanks"

"You do not recognize me do you?"

" I do not know you"

"We had a drink last year, where do you normally drink"

Well my local is the Fisherman`s Rest"

" That is it, that is were I met you" He was about seventy years old, short, grey hair parted in the middle, gold horned rimmed glasses and wearing a fawn overcoat looked like a Jew

"What are you doing these days?" "I have been buying and selling property"

"Do you need any pewter?"

"How do you mean, pewter?"

" Money old boy, let us find a quiet corner."

We moved over to the end of the bar.

"A colleague of mine has a large hotel in Chester, he has some spare cash, £200,000 in fact which he wants to lend out but it must be secured on property, it is not hot money just hidden from the tax man"

"If you are interested, meet me at the Prince of Wales tomorrow, oh by the way, I am Sir Sydney Patrick Rawlinson Caine M.M. M.C D.S.O. and Bar"

We shook hands " I am Eddie O`Brien"

"My brother also got the D.S.O. you know Eddie he got his Dick Shot Off at Dunkirk, well cheerio Edward I will see you tomorrow."

He was well oiled. I got to the Prince of Wales, spot on 1 o`clock, it was quite empty except for a few old dears having lunch, Sir Sydney was standing at the bar.

" I am glad you have come, how nice to see you again, you would not believe how difficult it is to lend large amounts of money and get adequate security for it, will your property value up?"

" Yes, Owen Oystens valued it at £330,000"

"

"Good, good, I will ring him up now and arrange a meeting for tomorrow, are you free tomorrow?"

" Yes, most of the day" He went to the reception to ring up, came back a few minutes later, "I have spoken to him Edward, it is all systems go, he is coming over at 1pm tomorrow, will you be able to get the deeds?"

"Once I have the money I can get the deeds off the bank"   "

Right Edward, I have to go now, I have another appointment, I will meet you here tomorrow, cheerio"

We met again the next day as arranged. "Let us sit over there by the window, keep your eye open for a white Rolls Royce."

Sir Sydney called the waiter over and ordered two double whiskies, It was now 1.30pm, " He is a bit late Edward must be the traffic."

At 1.45pm, the Hotel tannoy came on, " There is a phone call for Sir Sydney Patrick Rawlinson Caine, please come to reception."

" That is for me Edward." He returned after a few minutes.

"That was him Edward, Roger, has been delayed, business meeting, he said he would come across tomorrow instead, is that alright with you? I tell you what Edward why not meet me tonight, we will have a drink at the Clifton Hotel on the Promenade."

I met him at 9 o`clock, he was good company, said he had lived for many years in Knightsbridge, London, while we were standing at the a man came over and said to Sir Sydney.

"Have you got the time Sydney? You should have, you have done plenty" Sir Sydney just laughed,

"He is a real card, I was at Oxford with him".

At closing time, he said, "Do you fancy some supper?"

We walked around the corner to a Chinese café, the waiter came over, "Good evening Sir Sydney" he showed us to a table near the window, after the meal the waiter came over.

"Would you put this on my account please?"

"Certainly, Sir Sydney" The next morning I called in at Bates building suppliers depot, Henry Reynolds a member of staff, came out of the office at the rear, he said, "Hi Eddie, do you know who you were drinking with last night in the Clifton?"

"Do you mean Sir Sydney?"

"I mean Sir Sydney rip off, he is a con man, he is done 33 years in jail, he is a real Sir, married into a titled family and they paid him off, this was years ago, he is one of the best con men in the country.

He used to drink with the Great Train Robbers, he is mentioned in Bruce Reynold`s book "Autobiograpy of a Thief".

In the 1950`s he used to operate on the South of France, he was introduced to Lord and Lady Docker and invited on board their yacht, was introduced to the captain and the crew and being a good con man, he remembered all the names. The Dockers were away the following day.   Sir Sydney found a buyer for their yacht at £20,000, a bargain, he brings the buyer down, shows him around, introduced him to the crew, nails a bill of sale to the mast and the deal is done, he got five years for that in a French prison.

Another time in Liverpool Crown Court, he came up before Judge Laski, who was renowned for handing out stiff sentences.

Sir Sydney was expecting six to eight years but Judge Laski only gave him four. " Sydney Caine, I sentence you to four years in prison"

Sir Sydney said, under his breath, "I can do that standing on my head" but unfortunately the Judge heard him and replied,"

Here's another four years, do that when you get back on your feet, take him down."

Later on, the Judge brought Sir Sydney back and told him not to pass comment after being sentenced and just do the four years.

"So Eddie, be warned, watch your back".

I met Sydney the next day, he was sitting by the window,

"Nice to see you Edward, I have bought you a double scotch, he should be hear soon, keep your eye open for a white Roller. "

"Who is driving it Dick Turpin?"

"I do not know what you mean."

"What I mean is that there is no Rolls Royce, there is no one coming, you are a con man, you little shit, I have nothing you can con me out of."

" Oh dear the joke`s on me, " he roared laughing, "Someone told me that you were loaded, buying half the Promenade, I`m really sorry Edward,   I only con the rich. I apologies profusely, let me get you another drink."   He was too old for me to punch his lights out. I could see the funny side now knowing the set up.

A few weeks later, I was in the Clifton Hotel on The Promenade when I spotted Sir Sydney at the bar with a couple. The man was about sixty with grey hair and of quite a big build.

The woman was younger, about thirty-five brown hair tall and slim. I was about to slip past them when he grabbed my arm.

"Let me introduce my friend. This is Edward O`Brien, one of the most prolific developers in Europe. This is Harold Bell and his good lady.

He played for Bolton Wanderers with Nat Lofthouse and Barrass. He was a marvellous footballer." We shook hands.

I remembered Nat Lofthouse because he broke Bert Trautman's neck in the Cup Final. I also remembered Harold Bell because he received the longest football ban for misconduct. Bell bought me a drink, he said that he had nightclubs in Scotland called the "Gay Gordon's" and was in partnership with Jock Stein and said he was always looking for premises to expand.

Sir Sydney said, "Edward has a wonderful site here on the Promenade, 7 hotels in one block".

Bell said, "Is it far?"

"It's just a few blocks away". It was still light so he suggested that we walk down and have a look. Bell and I walked down to Agincourt, "I have not got the keys with me but I can show you inside tomorrow."

I said. Bell gave the building a good inspection from the outside he crossed the road to look at the roof.

" I am very impressed   it's ideal for what I want, how much are you asking Edward?"

"£330,000".

"Is there any one else interested?"

"A couple of breweries are interested at the asking price."

We walked back to the Clifton Hotel. Sir Sydney said, "What do you think, Harold?"

" It's ideal for what I want, such a good position".

Then turning to me he said. "Have you eaten Edward?"

"No I was jut going"

"Well, I tell you what, come and have dinner with us later this evening. Bring your good lady wife, we would like to meet her. Meet us here at 9p.m."

I could not wait to get home and give Helen the news. Helen was very laid back with two feet on the ground.

"Not another con man is he?"

"No Helen, I remember when he was a footballer, I recognize his face".

We got to the Clifton at about 9p.m. the Bells were already at the bar, " I have booked a table at the Prince of Wales as this place is only three star and the whole evening is on me."

"Thank God for that," I thought as I only had twelve pounds in my pocket. We walked across to the Prince of Wales, Southport's top hotel. We went to the first floor restaurant, where a pianist was playing in background. We had a lovely meal and a bottle of Champagne. God knows how much it cost. Then we went back across to the Clifton about midnight.

We had a few more drinks but I was getting worried. As, he had not mentioned the site all evening.

Then he spoke. "Now, Edward down to business, I am very interested in your hotel block, how far have the breweries gone?"

"There is a contract out at £330,000 but they want planning for a pub and hotel complex."

"I will match their offer as long as I have your word. There will be no 'Dutch' auction and you will sell it to me, we will shake on it."

We shook hands, "Now to seal this deal, I will give 10% deposit tomorrow£33,000, I will meet you in the Nat West bank on Lord Street tomorrow morning, is that alright with you?"

"That is fine Harold", I could hardly contain my excitement. Helen and I were so happy and could not sleep. I arrived at the bank at 9.15, went in at 9.30 and I sat in the corner facing the door. 9.35 came and went, as did 9.40 and 9.50. Still there was no sign of Harold Bell. "Maybe he's slept in," I thought. I approached the counter. "Excuse me, has a Mr Bell made an appointment here this morning?" The clerk went and checked, there was no appointment. I thought I would give him until 10.15 but he didn't appear. I was fuming. It takes an awful lot for me to lose my temper, but when I do I could kill someone. "I'm going to rip this bastards head off."

I flew around to the Clifton Hotel and went to the reception. "Could you tell me what room Mr Bell is in please?"

"Mr Bell checked out at 8a.m. this morning," came the reply. I could not quite understand what was going on.

Helen was expecting me home with a bag of money. The only thing I could think of was that Bell thought I was another con man like Sir Sydney but why spend all that money on a meal?

I found out later that Sir Sydney had conned Bell`s brother out of £20,000 and borrowed his briefcase to put it in! Happy days

Two days later my solicitor Jack Coulthurst rang me and he said, "I have got some bad news for you. "

I thought that will be a change!".

" Your other bank has gone bust, Slater Walker, they have been taken over by another bank called First Fortune. They have written to say you are £4000 in arrears and are going to take action to repossess your house."

I tried all kinds of banks, and brokers. Mr McNamee at Johnson Fry, J Marshall of Thamesdale Finance, Garfield Hillman, London Indemnity and Twentieth Century and Arab banks.

What I did not realize was that F.N.F.C was not an established bank belonging to the old school tie brigade, no other bank wanted anything to do with it. Mr Hanman of F.N.F.C. told me to put the site on the market so I gave it to Sykes and Waterhouse, one of the biggest estate agents on Merseyide. A young man, called Steve Pilling came out and took all the details and priced it at £275,000. He advertised it overlooking the North Sea, instead of the Irish Sea, just a small error! I only got one offer of £100,000 from Woodvale Construction. Mr Hanman wrote and said he had got an offer through Dunlop Heywood of Manchester of £100,000. This would not clear the debt but he would look to me for the balance, or shortfall, if not he would make me bankrupt. Happy days.

Some time after this, I was having a pint in the Windmill pub. I met a chap called Bernard Monks from Manchester, he said he had some property, and had come over to sort a tenant out who had not paid his rent. I told him I had some property. A short time later he moved to Southport and we became good pals.

The Shepherds at 51 the Promenade kicked off again, they said if I paid them £100 a week, they would delay the bankruptcy, so I had to agree, hoping something would turn up That meant I could not pay the other mortgages, which I was already falling behind with.

Helen's aunt and uncle were having problems on the upkeep of their house at 98 Hall Street Southport. The house was in bad repair and it was being repossessed. I agreed to buy the house off them but I would have to sell it before I could buy it, meaning that, I would have to complete with them and the new buyer on the same day.

I moved them into a flat at 21 Leicester Street. I started work on the house, some of my pals were helping out until I could pay them.

There was a young roofer working on the house, he asked me when I was moving in, I said that I was not moving in but that it was for sale. He said he wanted to buy a house but he had no deposit. I said that I could get him a 95% mortgage and we could ghost the deposit.

The arrangement was, that he would say he had given me the 5% in cash to hold the house for him. I got £6,500 and made £1,000 after paying everyone.

There was another house over the road for sale for £5,500, which been empty for some time according to the neighbours. The house had been left to the son who lived down South. I offered £4500 and asked for a key on exchange of contracts so I could get in and do the work then repeat the process.

That was, complete with the vendor and the buyer on the same day but this was refused.

I exchanged contracts and being desperate days, I broke in and started the work. This time I sold the house to a decorator, I made £1500 but the money was going out faster than it was coming in .

I spotted an article in the Daily Mail about a man in Yorkshire who was obtaining million of pounds of Arab money from Saudi Arabia.

His name was Reynolds. All the builders and property companies were obtaining loans to save them from bankruptcy through his contracts with the Arabs. His phone number was included so I rang him and asked for £200,000.

"No problem," he said but he needed a £200 fee for administration costs, I told him I would not pay up front fees.

"Do you think they would write an article in the Daily Mail if I was not genuine?"

In desperation I sent him the £200. A week later the Daily Mail rang and asked me if they could do a little article about the transaction.

I gave them brief details about the Agincourt site. A few days later I received a copy of the Daily Mail, there was a half page article, headlines were as follows: "Arabs on the Seafront at Southport".

The local paper, the Southport Visiter, rang up as they had seen it in the Daily Mail and they wanted some details. They did a full front-page spread with the following headline:

"Local Developer Seeks Arab Cash".

All my mates were calling me 'Mohammed O`Brien'. A few days later, the Daily Mail rang up asked me if I had thought about the name of the man with the Arab cash, "Doesn't the name Reynolds, ring alarm bells?"

I said "No"

"Well Reynolds is a Jewish name, how would he get cash off the Arabs when the whole Arab world hates the Jews!"

The reporter asked. "I am afraid you have been conned, with hundreds of other desperate builders".

This was my second bad experience with a Jew. My solicitor, dropped me when I ran out of money, now this bastard Jew robs me of £200.

About a week later I got a cheque for £200, apparently the Jew was visited by the police. He had paid all the money back he had stolen.

I was always told in business you need a tripod, three strong legs, a good solicitor, a good bank and a good accountant and all mine had failed me.

Hanman of F.N.F.C. wrote and said that the offer had been withdrawn for the Agincourt site and he was to instruct the bank`s solicitors to make formal demand on me and make me bankrupt and he wanted me to come down to the head office in London and so I went a few days later to Head Office at Finsbury Pavement London.

We sat down and started discussions.

"How much is your house worth?" I knew what was coming,.

"Not a lot, I only paid £15,500,"

"I have information here that it is a detached with twelve bedrooms with an acre of land by the Royal Birkdale Golf Club, I want a second charge on it and put it on the market the proceeds of the sale will come to us."

"Where am I going to live?"

" That is your problem.

" I had to think quickly "What about the tenants?"

"What tenants, you have never mentioned them before?"

"You never asked, I have six tenants upstairs in separate bed-sits and they all have a three year lease." I retorted.

He looked at me with disdain. "I will instruct a local valuer and if there is any equity on the property it will be sold, that I all for now."

"Thank you very much." On the train home I was thinking what to do, as there were no tenants in the house. The next day I went and bought six Yale locks and six numbers and put them on the bedroom doors.

The day the surveyor came I put six bottles of milk in the entrance hall. He came from Sykes Waterhouse. I told him all the tenants were out at work and I never went into their rooms when they were out. I showed him around the house and he said he must have a look in one of the flats I told him there was an old grumpy chap, up on the top floor and he was the only one in. It was my father-in-law Jasper, who was waiting in an empty room.

We went up to the second floor where Jasper was "lets see now flat 6" I knocked on the door "Could this gentleman have a look in your room?"

"No! He can't." and he slammed the door.

The surveyor asked, "What's the position with the bank?" "They want to evict us and sell the house." I explained. I told him about the Promenade and that the bank had gone bust. It was the bank's fault that I was now in this predicament

So being a good Scouser he must have put a low valuation on it. Hanman didn`t press the matter but he was still putting £10,000 penalties on for every extra two months extension which I had to agree to or be made bankrupt. As the months went by, the debt was escalating. I was up against the wall now. These were desperate days. would have to make another trip to London to seek finance and I decided to leave at once. "I am off now Helen, should be back early evening." 'Have you got everything Eddie, plans, papers, car keys?' 'Yes thanks Helen.' 'Good luck then Eddie, you will need it today.' I gave her a quick peck on the cheek. I started up my old Rover P4 and headed for Lime Street station Liverpool to catch the train to Euston. I bought the Financial Times and boarded the 9.40 a.m. train for London. The first class compartments were full of business executives and budding entrepreneurs. They were all ordering their late breakfast. It was July 1975. I was going to meet a Mr Spicer, a finance broker, or financial consultant, as they like to be called. I sat down at an empty table in the second class compartment. I took my papers and plans out of my inside pocket and laid them on the table. This was one of the most important days of my life. Mr Spicer had said that after half a dozen phone calls, and sending him details of the business proposition and projections that he could refinance my borrowings.

Two banks I had dealt with had already become insolvent in 1974. One was the First National Finance Corporation and the other was Slater Walker. I had never heard of a British bank going bust before. But I had to be in both of them. You may have heard the old saying 'as one door shuts another one slams in your face'. If I didn't get the refinance today I would lose everything I would be bankrupt and homeless!

I was first introduced to the First National Finance Corporation in 1972 by Mr Tim Woods of Southport Insurance Brokers.

My cousin Christopher Larkin of Target Life Insurance Company introduced me to Slater Walker. As I said both banks became insolvent. They don't call me Lucky Eddie for nothing. The train stopped at Runcorn, then Crewe, then we went speeding on to Euston, London. I looked at the FinanciaL Times FT Index. The First National's Finance Corporation shares had dropped from 200p to 1/2p. My head was spinning but I had to concentrate on my figures and get my presentation right, I really was in the mire. Property prices were going through the roof in the 1960's and early 70's, it had been the biggest property boom ever then the bubble burst and property prices plummeted.

The banks and insurance companies had lent millions on property. Flat developments and building sites were now not worth a carrot. Mine was only a pittance compared to some of the big property speculators who were limited companies. They went bankrupt not owing a penny because they were limited companies.

Unfortunately I was a sole trader with my house in the bank as collateral. Feeling a little peckish I walked down to the dining car and bought myself a cup of tea and a Kitkat. "This is the life for a tycoon!" I thought.　　　The train arrived at Euston Station just after noon. I had plenty of time to get to the hotel to meet with Mr Spicer at 1 p.m. I thought I would ring Helen and let her know I had arrived safely.

"Hi Helen it is me, I've just arrived at Euston. I just thought I would give you a ring. Is everything all right?"

I heard a big sigh. "Well it was until 11 am when the gas board came and cut the gas off".

"Oh Jesus I thought we had a few more days".

"Don't worry Eddie we have still got the electric".

"I'm sorry Helen I will see you later, lets hope things go well today."

I walked round to the hotel. It was packed with tourist　and businessmen. It was now spot on 1 o'clock. I had never met Mr Spicer before. I was looking for someone who I thought was looking for someone if you know what I mean. I went over to the reception and asked them to page Mr Spicer. "Excuse me I'm waiting for Mr Spicer, I wonder if you could page him for me, My name is O'Brien".

He was standing right next to me.

"Mr O'Brien pleased to meet you, Spicer is the name"

We shook hands; his handshake was limp and lethargic.

" Nice to put a face to a voice."

He was about 50 years old, stocky with a receding hairline and not very well dressed. It looked like he was wearing a demob suit.

We found an empty table in the corner of the lounge and sat down both sizing each other up. I could not ask him if he wanted a drink in case he asked for a double brandy. Furthermore I don't think I had enough for two coffees. God knows how much they cost in here! I had better sit him out.

At last he said, "Would you like coffee Mr O'Brien?"

He called the waitress over. She looked like a young Dolly Parton.

"A pot of coffee please beautiful. Now Mr O'Brien lets get down to business. Perhaps you could give me some history of the project and your good self".

I got my plans and papers out and laid them on the table.

Well, I was a butcher by trade, and in 1965 when I was 25. I started to buy houses which I split into small flats and bed-sits. I obtained 7 or 8 mortgages from different building societies. When I had an enough income I then became a full time landlord and quit the Butcher's trade in 1970. Since I had moved from Liverpool in 1967 to Southport, which is a seaside resort, I had noticed this large hotel called the Agincourt at 47/48 The Promenade, Southport. It had been lying empty for the past 15 years. I approached the First National Finance Corporation through Southport Insurance Brokers for the finance to purchase the hotel at £22,500.This was a fortune to me as I had in the past only paid up to £5000 for properties. My plan was to convert the Agincourt Hotel into 14 self-contained flats. There were grants available at £3000 per flat, a total of £42,000. Which would have covered the cost of the conversion. I would rent the flats out to increase my portfolio. Mr Michael Hanman was the gentleman I dealt with at their head office at First National Finance Corporation at Finsbury Pavement. He was not interested in the conversion. When he saw the plan of the whole site, a block of 7 hotels on one site overlooking the sea with panoramic views across to Blackpool bay. Mr Hanman then asked me what I wanted to be in the future, a landlord or a developer and that his associates had looked at the great potential of this site. They reckoned a new block; newly built of 72 flats on stilts with car parking underneath would be a very viable proposition. "Would you like to have a go at that? How much do you think it will cost?" I did not have a clue, being a butcher so I said about £1,000,000. "Well you're not too far out with your estimation Mr O'Brien. Come on fill your boots" A good northern expression as Mr Hanman originated from Manchester. "Do you want to have a go?" Without hesitation I said, "Yes, I will have a go.

"Good they will sell like hotcakes. Now you go along and buy the rest of the block. We will give you 90% of the purchase price. You put 10% down plus we will give you 100% of the redevelopment costs."

I could not comprehend why they would give me an open cheque when all I wanted was £22,500. What I did not know was that First National Finance Corporation was lending vast amounts of money to anybody. The only criteria was that they were breathing!

After about 6 months I had purchased 7 out of the 8 hotels. Then I exchanged contracts on the last one. Number 51 the Promenade for £40,000. I put £4,000 down then my solicitor Edgar Morris asked First National Finance Corporation for the balance of £36,000.

They wrote back and said that they had gone insolvent. My other bank Slater Walker went bankrupt not long after. The waitress finally appeared with the coffee. We both poured our own coffee out.

The hotel now was getting quieter after the lunchtime rush.

Mr Spicer seemed to be losing interest. He kept eyeing up the big blonde waitress.

"Did you follow that Mr Spicer?"

"Oh yes, yes very interesting, how much do you need in total for the whole project?"

I got my figures and passed them across the table. I knew them off by heart, after meeting so many bank managers and brokers and being turned down.

I require £300,000 to take out the banks and convert the hotels into 35 flats, as was my original intention. Don't forget there is a lot of interest added by First National Finance Corporation. We were both locked in the site, First National couldn't sell the site so they let the interest roll up after a while I had to pay £10,000 penalties for 56 day extra time or they would make me bankrupt if I did not accept the penalties.

My interest now must be accruing or rolling up at £1,000 per week.

He went silent for a while working out the "Yes I think I have a source for you. It could be a foreign bank does that matter?"

"Any bank in a storm Mr Spicer. I don't care where the money comes from."

"I don't see any problem, I can sort this out in the next 7 days."

I could have kissed him. Feeling so relieved and happy I could not wait to ring Helen with the good news.

"Now Mr O'Brien lets talk fees. It is a very difficult case to place let us say 2% of the total figure of £300,000. That is £6,000 is that OK?"

That is fine by me". I said not wanting to sound too elated.

"There is just one other matter Mr O'Brien, that is the administration fee of £200, I need that today."

"Administration fee? I asked you about up front fees last week you said that there weren't any. I would not have travelled all this way down if there were 'up front fees'

"Mr O'Brien, this is not an 'up front fee'."

"If it is before the loan it is an 'up front fee'. I will give you a irrevocable undertaking of my solicitor to pay you £6,000 out of the new loan plus your £200 administration fee."

"I am sorry Mr O'Brien we cannot proceed any further without the fee. I cannot work for nothing."

"£6,000 is not nothing for a few phone calls. So you are letting go of £6,000 in 7 days for the sake of £200 today."

I was thinking to myself this man is a con man. If you pay broker fees up front you never hear from them again. I know because in desperation I have done this before. The brokers can see you clutching at straws. They will still take the last coppers off you. Bastards.

I felt myself getting angry, very angry. I had £2.84 in my pocket and this bastard wants £200. A wasted journey I was boiling with rage.

"I think you are a conman!" I barked at him.

He stood up quickly and gathered his papers. He practically ran out of the hotel.

After a few minutes I headed back to Euston Station. I felt really down. The Liverpool train was at the platform. It was quite empty.

I sat with my head in my hands leaning on the table, what do I do now. I couldn't ring Helen and give her such devastating news I would have to tell her face to face. My head was 'cabbaged' as I thought,.

How am I going to tell Helen and our boys. We could be out in the street. Had I been too ambitious, too greedy trying to play with the big boys. Why didn't I stay in the meat trade? We had and no hassle.

The more you own the more you have to worry about.

But talk like that is no good, no one gives you anything in this life, you have to go and get it. You have to put your head on the line otherwise we would all be living in council flats working for the council. Living in the poverty of socialism. The only chance a socialist takes is crossing the road. When you were a kid and you got into trouble you would run to your Mam and she would put her arms around you and cuddle all your cares away. God I could do with her now!

The train pulled out of the station I should be back in Liverpool by 6 p.m. and should be home about 7 p.m. I sat there thinking what could I do. There was nothing really. I'd tried dozens of banks and financial institutions. They didn't want to take First National Finance Corporation out because it was not one of the banks belonging to the establishment. Usually when banks get into difficulties other banks step in and bail them out but not this one.

The train was now approaching Runcorn, next stop Liverpool, then home to Southport, I was thinking just what I could do, which way to turn. There was no answer, I felt really frustrated and desperate, and I had had enough. It was Hanmans letter saying that he had been patient enough and was going to foreclose on the loan that had made this journey to London necessary, I was dreading giving the news to Helen.

I passed the Fisherman`s Rest .Into Westbourne Road and turned into the drive, the house was in total darkness. God! They must have cut the electric off as well. I opened the front door, Shane, our golden retriever came pounding towards me, I made a fuss of him.

Helen came out of the lounge with a torch, "Yes they have both been today Eddie"

When you get your gas and electric cut off you would think it could not get any worse but it can and it does, Helen could see by my face that it was bad news,

"Sorry Helen, just another wasted trip, one of many"

"What happens now?" We walked into the lounge, lit by a candle on the mantlepiece, " I cannot even make you a cup of tea Eddie"

"Never mind, we have not got the bankruptcy writ off Hanman yet, it will take a month or two to get to court. We have probably got six to eight weeks before we get evicted."

The next day I went 'over the water' to Greasby where my brother George had his butcher's shop and borrowed the money to put the gas and electric back on.

The following week, I read in the paper that the big five banks had taken over First National Finance Corporation.

It was now April 1975. I wrote to them because they would have new managers and personnel and Hanman would have left. I asked could I go back to the original idea of converting the hotels into flats as no one wanted to buy the site for development and the only way out for both of us was to go back to my original plan.

We would now get a total of 35 flats. If we could average £11,000 per flat, that would be a total of £385,000. They asked me to come down to London to discuss the matter, the trip was successful and they gave me a facility of £25,000 to start the Agincourt Hotel conversion into 14 flats.

I asked for tenders for the work, the lowest price was £61,000, which was quite a shock.

My architect, Brian Marsden, found a building firm he had used before, G&N Builders, they quoted £28,000 so they got the job.

They gave me a float of £3000 then we had to complete the work and get stage payments. We completed the first 14 flats in twenty weeks then I had to sell six of the flats before we could get any money to do the next six.

So work stopped completely. I used two estate agents, Edward Jackson, manager Dave James and Entwistles, manager Andy Coburn but they only valued the flats between £8000 and £11000 and thought the back ones would be hard to sell. It was now approaching Christmas and my mother-in-law suggested we spend it with them in Port Elizabeth, South Africa.

All that we needed was the airfare. I sold my van, scaffolding, concrete mixer and other materials and bought the tickets. I was determined for us to have a holiday, come what may. I had just bought the plane tickets when I got a writ for repossession of our home at Westbourne Road. It was from First Fortune who had taken over Slater Walker. The writ said I owed £28,500, I had only borrowed £12,500 and I knew I was £4000 in arrears.

I rang my solicitor; Jack Coulthurst and he said that they had compounded the interest. I told him I had just booked tickets to go to my in-laws in South Africa. He said that he would go to County Court about the house and I might as well go to South Africa because if I have no money to pay I would probably lose the house if I was there or not.

I was having a drink with my mate Bernard Monks, I told him about the house and that it might be re-possessed and with arrears I owed nearly £20,000 but it was worth £50,000. I told Bernard I was thinking of selling it to my sister in law, Sylvia Bent who was in South Africa but I would need a job on paper to get her a mortgage. It would be easy to get one on that valuation.

"Could I put her down working for you, to get the loan?"

He had bought a small Estate Agency called John Taylors on Lord Street, which collected rents.

"I don't think so, I have a business to run"

"So you are going to see us out on the street then?"

"I won't do it, I am a business man"

"Well just give me a blank headed paper, I will fill it in myself and sign it"

" No I cannot do it"

"Thank you Bernard you are good friend"

Helens parents had emigrated a couple of years ago to South Africa with their daughter Rita and family and brother Reg. Jasper had been home a couple of times in between. We were looking forward to the trip.

I asked my mate Bernard if he would go to court and if I lost the house, would he get the furniture out and store it in one of his flats, he said that he would.

We flew a week before Christmas from Gatwick to Amsterdam then boarded the KLM Jumbo Jet but because it was going to South Africa with the Apartheid Regime the plane couldn't fly over black Africa so we landed in Greece and then Lusaka and then to Johannesburg then down to Port Elizabeth, twenty two hours all together.

It was a beautiful country, Helen`s parents had a flat just near the beach and opposite the Elizabeth Hotel. The Blacks were very friendly. They liked the British but hated the Dutch Afrikaans who treated them like dirt. In the public building there were separate toilets for blacks and whites and the blacks had to go upstairs on the bus. It was like another world, no phone calls, no bailiffs, no hassle, we stayed for a month and had a wonderful time, we were actually tempted to stay for good but looking to the future for our sons, there were too much racial undertones. The Blacks hated the Whites, the Indians hated the Blacks and nobody liked the Coloureds. Jasper told me the tale about the Black African up in front of a White Judge, the Judge gave the African ten years for riding his bike with no lights and he said he was a lucky man, if it had been dark he would have got life. We stayed at the Zurburg Inn for a few days a little holiday village up in the hills, the waitress who served us over a couple of days was very efficient and looked after us.

Just before leaving I gave her a tip of five Rand, which was about £2.50, you would think she had won the pools, she was delighted, probably a week's wage for her. I rang Bernard to see how the court case had gone. It was good news. Bernard was sitting next to my solicitor in the courtroom so the judge thought he was me. My solicitor Jack Coulthurst did all the talking. The bank was represented By Victor Rose Solicitors from Manchester. The Judge agreed with my solicitor that the bank had no right to compound the interest so he adjourned the case for 28 days to allow the bank to get the figures right. It was nice to have a home to come back to. Reluctantly we had to return home from a beautiful but volatile country. Helen's parents said they were a bit worried about the future there and they were thinking of coming home to the U.k. 'Soft lad' said that they could come and stay with us until they found somewhere.   After being home for a week everything had ground to a halt as I had to sell six flats before I could have more cash to do the next stage. I met another finance brokerage called Shaefer House from Crosby run by Ted Mcillvenna and Phil Shaw. They introduced me to Brokers Crystal House at Bootle but no funds materialized I was having a pint with Ted and Phil in the George at Crosby and they said that they were going to the Liverpool "Sound Studio" at Kirkby.

One of their clients was trying to raise funds to get a record produced called SHANKLY a tribute to the legendary manager of Liverpool Football Club who had just retired. A woman called Peggy Carroll had written the songs and approached Dave Roylance of Liverpool Music Management. They said that I could come along and listen in and I agreed.

They had booked the Liverpool Police Choir to sing as they do on the 'Kop' but they failed to show up. Because they had not been paid. After waiting a hour the engineer on the tape deck suggested that the six of us there should sing with the tape. As the music was already recorded, we would then sing with the tape again and again until it sounded like thousands on the "Kop".

I was useless! Nobody had sung before. People were coughing and it came out on the tape some one suggested we all go for a pint and loosen up. We came back a few hours later and recorded both songs the B side A Little Bit Of Scotland and A Tribute to Shankly.

It was played back to us. With the music it sounded great, mind you we had had six pints. Dave Roylance the producer suggested we all put £500 in and get the record cut, we all agreed. 10,000 records were cut and the sleeves were designed and printed at C.B.M of Bold Street

We went live on Radio City to promote the Shankly record.

They were very helpful but Radio Merseyside did not want to know.

That little snide Billy Butler would not play the Shankly record.

We sent him 3 copies but he said that he had lost them all. He killed the record not playing it on Radio Merseyside

I felt this was an insult to a great man who earned the respect of every Merseyside football fan either red or blue.

Woolworth`s said that they would sell the record if they were the only distributors and not sold anywhere else.

This was agreed, we delivered the records ourselves to Woolworth all over Merseyside. We were invited to Shankly's house he was 'made up' and over the moon. He kept playing it over and over he was delighted and very moved. It was a tribute to the greatest manager.

The strange thing was that we could not get it played at Anfield.

We asked Dave Roylance when he wanted our £500 he said that he did not need it now, and was cutting us out.

Which turned out well as the record was a flop. It was not marketed or promoted properly. The record went into Woolworth but they were not coming out. It was crap to be honest.

The flats were still not selling on the Agincourt site. I rang F.N.F.C and asked if I could get the front of 47 /48 Tarmaced it would look better when the punters came to view. The estimate was £900 and they agreed get the work done and send the bill in.

I got my Tarmacer Paddy, a Scouser who had done jobs for me before. To do the job he wanted paying in cash but he would give me a receipt to send to the bank, which I did. Few days later I was standing at the front of the site when a rather large gentleman came over

"Mr O`Brien, I am Mr Garner head Bailiff, Southport Council. You are wanted at the town hall a little matter of rates we have sent you 17 summonses you have ignored them."

"I have been busy"

"

"You won't be to busy to go to gaol will you? Come with me to the town hall."

At the town there were a couple of gentleman from the rates and finance office they said rates were still due from the hotels going back 2 years and from various properties.

I explained that 2 banks had gone bust and I had just got going again. I had created 14 new flats on the promenade so I had increased their income. When I finished the block they would have 35 new ratepayers increasing their income tenfold. And I was also building homes for people, which the council were not doing in Southport.

They were not impressed. "Mr O`Brien you owe us £2,000 we want it now".

"Well I have not got it, I am doing my best to keep going and to pay everyone."

"Do you know you can go to prison for non-payments of rates? For now, we will take your goods starting with your furniture. We will be in touch, good-day."

When I got home there was a letter from the A Dean and D Dean, Sherriff of Liverpool they had a warrant to sell my personal assets for some rates I had not paid in Bootle.

Helen had been going for regular smear test over the years she had been for one today and they seemed very concerned and told her she had to go back tomorrow for further tests.

The new court date was next Monday for the house repossession.

You would not think things could get any worse but they do.

Helen returned from the clinic the next day very upset they said she had cancer of the uterus and would have to go into hospital as soon as there was a bed available they had made mistakes in the smear procedure

The town hall rang they were coming for our furniture a week on Tuesday. This would give me a week to find the rates money.

I rang Jack Coulthurst to confirm the court date for repossession he said it was a week on Monday but if I had nothing to pay into the court he feared the worst, which would be eviction".

I told him that the bailiffs were coming to take the furniture he said that there was nothing he could do about it.

On Friday the tarmacer Paddy came for his £900.

"Nothing has come through yet paddy, I will ring them now while you're here."

"Hello could I speak to Mr Glover?" there was a few moments silence.

"I am afraid that Mr Glover is no longer with the bank," was the reply!
"He was with the bank before it was taken over he was one of the last to go, what is the problem?"
"The problem is that Mr Glover had given me the go ahead to get the forecourt tarmaced on the Agincourt site at Southport. I have sent in the receipt for £900. I have the gentleman here waiting for his money it should have come today".
"Oh dear! There is nothing here in writing everything has to go through the board. I will put it on the agenda for next week. How is that?"
I looked at paddy he was snarling.
"Get the fucking money my men are outside and they want their wages". "Hello," I said to the voice on the other end of the 'phone.
"That is no good the gentleman is sitting here waiting. Could you wire £900 through to the bank in Southport?"
"I am afraid not everything has to be sanctioned at board level you will have it next week, Good bye."
Paddy was up on his feet, his lips curled back, teeth like a Rotweiler.
"So you have not got the money, you are in deep shit, deep trouble"
"Are you threatening me?"
"No I am promising you, I will break your fucking legs."
With that he stormed out. I was having a pint with Bernard and a couple of the lads in the London 'early doors'. I left at 8 p.m. I was home for ten past, Bernard rang to say 3 men had came in looking for me I missed them by seconds as they left they said " Don`t worry we will get him", seems like Paddy wants to keep his promise.
The hospital rang and informed Helen that there were no beds available in Southport, but she could get into Ormskirk Hospital. As it was urgent they booked her in for Wednesday.
Next week looked like a bad week.
1. Tuesday funiture repossessed.
2 Monday repossessed
3Wednesday, Helens cancer operation.
4 Paddy trying to break my legs.
What happens if we are evicted on Monday? Do they throw the furniture in the garden? What if Paddy breaks my legs before Wednesday? We will both be in hospital and who will look after the children and no home to come back to. Time seemed to drag over the weekend waiting for the court case I had nowhere to turn, no money to pay in.   But it is no good feeling sorry for yourself.
You have to fight on or you go under. A quitter never wins and a winner

never quits.   Who am I kidding? I arrived at the
Southport County Court 5 minutes early at 1.55 p.m. Could I find a
parking space? I went around the block a couple of times and ended up
about ½ mile away. I started to run.   It was 2 p.m. already. I
entered the court building. By now it was nearly ten past, I looked down
the corridor they were coming out it was all over. I just stood there,
shattered, when Jack Coulthurst came within range.   He winked at me
"Don't panic Eddie" We got out to the pavement,   "You are one
lucky man, when we got in to court the other solicitor handed the writ to
the judge and said. "This case your Honour, is Slater Walker v E&H
O`Brien but it should have been First Fortune v E& H O`Brien."
I pointed this out to the judge, he agreed with me it was the wrong
name on the writ, so lucky for you it has been adjourned for 28 days".
"Thanks Jack, you are a marvel. I can't thank you enough,.
Helen will be delighted" The first phone box that I came to I rang Helen
with the good news. On the way home, I thanked almighty God and Our
Lady for the good result that I'd had today and would they help me
tomorrow. Even though you don't go to church as often as you should
you never lose your faith.
The bailiffs turned up at 10p.m. the next day 3 of them with their
clipboards. They wanted to itemize everything before the vans came.
Helen was not feeling too good and had taken painkillers.
She was resting on the settee; the three bailiffs started at the top of the
house and were working their way down.
"I had better make you a cup of tea Helen in case they take the kettle".
One of the bailiffs came down into the kitchen. He was looking out of
the window at the back garden. "Have you got any garden furniture Mr
O`Brien?"
"No". "Have you got a lawn mover?"
"No"
"There is one out there in your garden"
"That belongs to next door, I borrowed it"
"Will they verify that in writing?"
"I would think so, you are not taking the lawn are you?"
This gave me an idea. Just them the doorbell rang. There were three
men standing there. "We are bailiffs from Dean & Dean of Liverpool. We
have a 'Walking In' possession order for your goods and chattels"
"You will have to get in the queue mate, the Southport bailiffs are
already here".
They pushed past. The other three bailiffs were in the front lounge

"What is going on here, we have come from Liverpool to claim O`Briens furniture."

"We have already claimed it. We are from Southport Council."

Mr Dean said, " Well I am afraid you cannot have it. I am the sheriff of Merseyside & Cheshire and I have higher authority than you, so we are taking them".

"No we are taking them we were here first."

There were six of them squaring up to each other. The two who were talking were prodding each other in the chest.

"I hope they kick off." I thought. I was standing in the doorway hoping some one would throw a punch.

"Excuse me I am just the owner I would just like to say that I don't own the furniture, it is my house, but all the furniture belongs to my wife's parents who live here with us.

At present they are on holiday in South Africa and won't be home until next week." That calmed things down a bit,.

" Can you get that in writing Mr O`Brien? I am Mr Dean, I have higher authority than these gentlemen."

"Yes I can get that in writing as soon as they come home".

"Good. You have 28 days to comply."

They all left glaring at each other. Thank God my prayers had been answered again. The next day Wednesday I drove Helen out to Ormskirk Hospital at lunch time I could see the apprehension on her face she seemed very tense and nervous, which was to be expected.

Helen was soon allocated in a ward, she asked me to go and ask the Indian lady doctor if she had to have this operation. I went down to office at the end of the ward, the doctor said it was vital she had a hysterectomy or the cancer would spread and kill her. I went back and held her hand

"I am sorry love but you have to have the operation to make you better". Helen had the operation the next day, I went to see her in the evening, she was still a bit drowsy and now and again grimacing with pain, it is hard to watch some one you love in such pain. I did not stay to long so she could get some rest, the Indian doctor said the operation was a success and Helen would soon be on the road to recovery.

I called in at the "Railway" in Ainsdale for a quiet pint I was keeping out of my local in case Paddy's thugs turned up. About half an hour later an old pal of mine turned up, Sammy from Crosby. I had not seen him for quite some time. He was on crutches his right leg in plaster.

"Sit down there Sam I will get you a pint."

"Lager please Ed"

"What happened to you then Sam? "I got run over"

After a few more pints he told me he had not got run over and that he had upset some business colleagues and they had put a contract out to break his leg.

He said three men picked him up two held him down and the third broke his leg with a sledgehammer. They said it was nothing personal, just doing a job. I told him about my trouble with Paddy.

He said, "Don't try and fight them they are professionals if they don't get you they will break your wife's legs."

"I am not trying to fight them I am trying to dodge them until the money comes through."

When I awoke the next morning I made myself some tea and toast, I sat there thinking, I had better ring Paddy and ask him for a bit more time. Then I thought I better ring the bank and see when this money was arriving. No joy but it would be on the agenda next week!

"Hello Paddy it is Eddie O'Brien".

"Have you got the money? It's no good ringing me if you have not got the fucking money"

"I have just rung the bank they said that the money would be here next week".

"It is no fucking good next week you twat you will get sorted in the next few days even if we have to come to your house"

"Look Paddy can I come down to see you just for ten minutes, I have always paid you before, just give us ten minutes."

There was a short silence, "O.K I will meet you in the Liver, corner of South Rd at 12 o'clock.'

I got to the pub spot on twelve, he was standing at the bar.

"What are you having"

"Just half a bitter please Paddy"

He motioned me to the table in the corner we sat down. I could not pick my drink up my hands were shaking I was expecting the three thugs to come in.

"Now shoot and don't give me any shit."

He was in his late fifties short and stocky with dark brown hair brushed back. He wore a brown striped suit with matching brown striped tie he did not do any physical work himself.

"I have a few problems at the moment Paddy,"

"Like what?" "

"Well last Monday I was in court at Southport they are repossessing my house, I have 28 days before I am evicted. Tuesday the bailiffs are coming to take the furniture, Wednesday my wife Helen had a life or death operation for cancer they have cut her womb out. I have 5 bankruptcies to sort out 35 county court summons and you are chasing me trying to break my legs."

I could not speak anymore as my voice was shaking. There was a long silence. I could see that he was moved.

His eyes were filling up. " Fucking hell," he said.

"Come with me" We started to walk up South Rd. I was still expecting to get jumped. We entered the Midland Bank.

"Sit there" he pointed to the chair by the door and went over to the counter.

"Right let us go back to the Liver." Our drinks were still there I had not touched mine. A few more people had come in.

"I have been a right bastard, you must have the heart of a lion. I would have topped myself by now all that worry and stress."

He put his hand in his inside pocket, "Here take this £2,000 it will help to keep a roof over your head, pay me back when you can,
God Bless You."

Scousers salt of the earth. "Thanks Paddy you are a gem you have saved my life I will never forget you for this. I won`t let you down".

I called in at the hospital to see how Helen was she was sitting up and was delighted with the news of Paddy's generosity.

Helen came home a week later she had to take things easy and not lift anything .

I paid a £1000 of the rates and paid a £1000 off the arrears on our house to First Fortune and they said we could have 3 months to sought it out Good news at last from the estate agents.

They had offers on 3 of the flats at Agincourt. I was going to the site every day and I put up a sign, 'OPEN TO VIEW'. I was standing on the second floor looking across the bay. I could see Blackpool Tower in the distance. The flats did have wonderful views I looked down and saw that there was a couple coming on to the site. I ran down stairs three at a time. They were a elderly couple, she was tall slim very elegant and had that Dolly Blue rinse in her hair, she was carrying a pekingese dog.

He was shorter, wearing a blazer with a anchor on the badge grey flannels and a sea captains cap, probably off the boating lake.

"Good afternoon we would like to view but we have not got an appointment have we Charles?"

"Don`t worry I think I can fit you in. follow me. We will take the lift to the top floor and show you the magnificent views across estuary they out of this world." I eagerly explained to them. We got in the lift.

The woman turned to me and asked, " What is your name young man?"

"Edward, " I replied. A bit of class, here I thought.

"Edward could you hold Bobby my little dog. Bye the way this is Captain Charles and I am Gai". Bobby licked my face. His breath stank.

I showed them the whole 14 flats, then they stood outside looking up.

"You know Charles, I think we should buy 6 on the front."

0 I thought I was hearing things. He was non-committal. The only comment he made was "I see that there is no fire escape Edward"

"Well yes but the Fire Station is only around the corner".

"Come on Bobby come to Mummy. We are looking for a investment for our capital, we will have to think about it and come back to you".

About a week later she came back on her own with just Bobby.

"I am afraid my friend the sea captain is not interested. Have you got any larger flats 2 bedrooms for me and Bobby, those you showed me are a bit small." "I have some bigger luxury flats on the corner at no 45, they are very spacious with beautiful views, but I have not started them yet I have to sell some of the other flats first, cash flow you now."

"Can you show them to me? Will you hold Bobby he likes you?"

His breath was terrible then he started farting. I showed her the 3 floors at 45 they were huge 18 to 20 feet square high ornate ceilings.

I could see she was impressed.

Then she spoke. "I like the ground floor. Bobby can go out for a wee at night."

"He is a beautiful dog, aren`t you Bobby" I said as he licked my face. I was nearly sick.

"How much would this one be?" she enquired.

"£12.950 and built to the same high quality standard as the others.

To be very honest with you Gai, my bank has gone bust and I am working my way out slowly"

"Edward I have sold my flat in Birkdale and don't want to lose my buyer, what if I lent you £5000 to get you started would that help?"

"I would have to think about it. Yes, that would be fine it would help."

She wrote a cheque out for £5,000. I rang F.N.F.C to see if it was all right to take the money they said take all you can the more the merrier.

I found a plumber Jack Priestly, a Yorkshire lad a bit of a all rounder. He said that we had better make the roof watertight as the building was over 100 years old and needed reproofing completely. It had to be stripped felted battened.

We had no scaffold so we had to climb through the attic and out of the skylight. We saved about half of the slates.

Jack estimated that we would need 5,000 slates with the felt and battens it would cost about £3000. Some of the joists needed replacing as well. All the materials arrived the next day,.

Jack said "Where are the rest of the lads?"

"There's only me and you Jack".

"Fuck me! I will go to the foot of our stairs. Right Ed, you carry them 5,000 slates up and I will bang them on. "

It took us a week to felt and batten, then I started carrying the slates up 10 at a time 500 trips up 3 floors through the attic and out on to the roof. I must have lost nearly a stone. After the roof was completed we started the ground floor for Gai and discovered woodworm in the floorboards and dry rot in the joists. The flat must have been 60 feet in length 18 feet wide a lot of timber to replace, the £5000 was soon gone but not a lot to show for it from Gai`s point of view. She came around the following Monday not impressed at all by the lack of progress. I took her across the road and showed her the roof. "

'We have put a new roof on altogether which cost us over £3,000 it will last a hundred years." I assured her. We went back into her flat, I showed her all the timber and new floorboards that had been replaced.

"Gai, it is no good putting kitchens and bathrooms in when the roof is like a sieve. I could have covered all this woodworm and dry rot with hardboard to finish off, but I am a great believer in 'do unto others as you would they would do unto you' and I have done a good job".

"Edward how much money have you got left?" she asked.

"Very little Gai."

I thought, I'd better stroke Bobby. He wagged his tail furiously

"He does like you Edward, here you hold him". Bobby licked my face, breath like a sewer.

"He is a little beauty, aren`t you Bobby"

"I can give you another £5000 that will help you. "She wrote out a cheque and handed it to me. " Than you very much Gai. I can crack on now with your flat come back in 3 weeks you will see a big difference".

"I only lent you the money because Bobby likes you Edward".

"He is a wonderful dog Gai there's no doubt about that.

" When she came back 3 weeks later we had put the kitchen in, bathroom and central heating in Gai was very impressed. As we were talking in the front lounge, a brown Rolls Royce pulled on to the car park. "Excuse me Gai" I went outside. An elderly lady and gentleman, immaculately dressed, got out of the car.

"Good morning can I help you " I put on my best salesman's voice.

" We are looking for a flat mainly for week ends for my hubby and I and our little dog, oh by the way can we have a dog in here?"

" You can have a elephant madam"

The couple were in their 'sixties'. You could see that they were loaded. I showed them around the first 14 flats. They liked them but said they were too small and did I have anything bigger.

"I have some spacious luxury flats on the end of the block but I can't start them yet until I sell some of these smaller ones".

"Could we have a look at them?"

"Certainly follow me." I took them up to the top floor at 45a above Gai`s. They thought the view was fantastic but to many stairs to climb.

"What about the ground floor?"

"I am sorry I have somebody on the ground floor. I can show you the first floor nobody has claimed that yet". They said they would like the first floor. I explained my predicament. We went downstairs and walked into Gai`s flat. Gai got up to greet them,

"I am Mrs Gai Hyde from Birkdale near the Royal Birkdale Golf Course you know."

"We are Mr & Mrs Hartley. We own Shore Sheet Metal in Oldham Manchester."

They all shook hands. "Beautiful Rolls you have Mr Hartley, I have a Mercedes Coupe. This is Edward O`Brien the developer.

Now Edward's bank has gone bust so you will have to give the lad some money to get on with it. I have just given him £10,000."

"How much do you need Mr O`Brien?" asked Mr Hartley

"Well I would have to do the top flat as well, as the services run through each flat". He got his cheque book out and wrote a cheque and handed it to me. "Here will that do it is for £9.000 ".

"That is great Mr Hartley you are a gentleman. Come back in a month's time you will see a big difference. Thank you very much".

When they went Gai said haughtily "Just because they have the brass it does not mean they have class"

"They will do for me Gai any day of the week".

I hired a joiner, Frank Healey. There were so many windows and I had to match the Georgian style in the other flats. Some of the windows were 8x4 feet and there were 27 in total they cost a fortune. I rang the bank again to see if it was all right to take more money, they told me to take any money that was offered. They would because it was increasing their security. The timbers were rotted. Wet rot, dry rot and woodworm. Some of the joists were 15 x3 inches it would have been cheaper to knock the building down and start from scratch. The 3 flats were finished now and they looked fantastic, I had no money left to paint the outside and tarmac the car park. Gai came around to inspect and my pal Bobby 'the best dog in the world', she was delighted.

"What about the outside painting Edward?"

"Well Gai with putting these luxurious bathrooms and kitchens in for you and fitted wardrobes I have spent all the money."

"I will lend you another £5000 that will be £15,000 in total but I will have to charge you 20% interest is that alright".

I had no choice but to agree.

" That's fine Gai" not as daft as she looks. I rang my mate Paddy.

I had since paid him the £900 I owed him, he charged me £1000 for the front of 45 & 46,I gave him £2000 and a £1000 off the £2000 he had so kindly lent me in my hour of need, we painted the outside ourselves. Gai and the Hartleys moved in they were very pleased. The agents had by now sold 4 flats all front ones. Out of the first 14 flats but the bank took all the money, so we had to stop work again.

Another viewer came the following day she wanted a 2 bedroom ground floor flat. "The only 2 bedroom flat is on the second floor".

"That is not suitable my husband he can't climb the stairs he has had a heart attack has angina asthma diabetes rheumatism and suffered a slight stroke and has epileptic fits"

"He is not a well man then"

I had to go back to go home to get some more planks it was about 2 o`clock I loaded the planks onto the van and was just about to drive off when Helen came around the rear of the house with a young man she looked quite shocked .

Oh oh oh er er I have just been out to lunch with Stevens friend my head was cabbaged at the time and I left , it is only when looking back you can see things clearly. I wonder why they went back into the house maybe for his afters etc

My mate Bernard said he had heard that there were two houses for sale for £400,48 &50 Warwick Southport, I went to have a look at them, they were both tenanted. Two up and two down no bathrooms, in a block of four. I called in to see Andy Coburn at Entwistle, he told me the rents were 38p per week. I said I would buy them if I could put £40 down and could I have 3 months completion he agreed.

"They belong to British Rail and they never rush things. By the way Ed I

have another 3 houses in Warwick Street, 9, 11 and 13 no.9 is vacant".
"How much are they Andy?"
"£2,100 for the vacant no.9 and £600 for the other 2."
"I will have them as well, but I need the same terms."
"It is a deal then Ed" I had to drag these purchases out as long as I could because I had no money to buy them. I asked the vendors' solicitors for a key so that I could get in and start work on no.9. I had to get a buyer before I could buy it myself. They refused. So I broke in and started work on the renovations. "These are desperate days, no one is going to help me, I have to sort it out myself."
Remember what the Yank insurance man said 'A Quitter never Wins and a Winner Never Quits'.
John Scarisbrick was a joiner who had worked for me before. I remember him saying he was looking for a house, so I went to see him.
"Are you still looking for a house John?"
"Yes but I have no deposit" "Don't worry about that John, I have a house 9 Warwick Street if you help me with the renovations you can have it for 90% of the building Societies valuation and I will pay your legal fees. We will ghost the deposit".
We worked all hours to get the house ready, the abbey National valued the house at £5,750 so I would get £5,175 less, both legal fees.
I could now pay for all the houses 11,13,48,50 Warwick Street not worth a lot and a income of £6;50 per week. I made about £1000 off the house so I gave it to Paddy the tarmacer to settle my debt.
The Sheppards at no 51 the promenade had restarted bankruptcy proceeding again, then out of the blue they informed me they had found a buyer for their Guest House at £33,000 with the £4000 I had give them they were getting a total if £37,000 when they had only paid £7,750 the year before.
I thought they would let me off with the £3000 I still owed or at least time to pay. Shepherd rang me and said" you have got 28 days to pay or you're bankrupt"
The rates office, at the Town Hall, were threatening me with prison again and I had other debts to pay.
The only thing I could think of was to sell no 11 Warwick Street to my sister-in-law, Sylvia Bent, who was in South Africa and pretend to the building society she was here and that the house was vacant.
Then just keep paying the mortgage it was the only way out.
I knew the tenant Mrs Ralph went to Ormskirk Market on a Wednesday so I arranged for the valuer to come then I told Mrs Ralph that the valuer

was coming for insurance purposes and could I wait in for him.
She agreed.

Desperate days! I did everything through a mortgage broker, used a different solicitor and everything done through the post.

Everything went according to plan. I used the Abbey National because they had valued next door no.9. I got about £5000. I asked the building society on behalf of my sister-in-law that the mortgage be paid through her bank account so no mail would go to the house.

A month later all hell broke loose! The building society sent a monthly payment book to no.11. Mrs Ralph sends it back. The next thing the building society manager was down asking who and where is Miss Sylvia Bent? Next day the solicitor I had used, Barry Davidson of Black and Davidson Solicitors from Liverpool, was on the phone.

"Get yourself down here at once you are in deep trouble selling tenanted property as vacant. I arrived at their Dale Street office,

"Now Mr O`Brien you are looking at a prison sentence here. You have borrowed £5,000 on a house you paid only £300 for last month would you call that sharp practice? I think the police would call it fraud.

But this is your lucky day, the Manager at the Abbey National is a close friend of mine, he only took over last month and does not want any problems. This is his first month so if you pay the £5000 back in 7 days that's the last you will hear about it, Good day"

As I was driving home I was thinking what do I do now I had paid Sheppards their £3000 and the rates £1000 so I only had £1000 left.

The next day I made an appointment at the Midland Bank at Formby to see Wilf Gill. He liked a liquid lunch so I went in the afternoon.

"I need £4000 Wilf. I can give you 3 houses as security."

"Nothing doing Eddie I hear you are having problems on the promenade".

"That is getting sorted now Wilf."

"Sorry Eddie can`t help"

My next Bank was the Natwest a Mr Knowlsen a real gentleman who had always helped in the past.

"MR Knowlsen could you lend me £4000? I can give you 3 houses as security"

"Sorry Mr O`Brien but I have had trouble with head office about your overdraft in the past and now they want your account in the black.
I am sorry I can't help you they are giving me hell".

"I might as well go throw myself in the Marine Lake"

Mr Knowlsen said, "I will come with you!"

I tried everywhere even went as far as Manchester. It was now Friday, my last day. I tried Barclays, Lloyds and T.S.B. in the morning, my last hope was Wilf Gill at the Midland in the afternoon.

"Not you again Eddie?"

"I am afraid so Wilf I am up against the wall. Come on Wilf it is only £ 4000." I told him what I had done.

"You always sailed close to the wind Eddie"

"I had to do it or go under, come on Wilf if I go to jail what about the £10,000 I owe you? That will go down the pan."

He took a cigarette out and lit the wrong end.

"You will have me in the nuthouse," he sighed.

He lit another cigarette took a few drags.

" O.K. Eddie, you can write a cheque for £4000 but this is the last".

"Could I have cash please Wilf I have to pay it in by 4 p.m.

I can't thank you enough Wilf you have saved my bacon."

I dashed down to Black and Davidson and paid the money in, I cannot take much more, but I knew I was going to. At last we have sold 6 flats out of the first 14 so F.N.F.C lent me another £23,000 to convert 6 flats at 46 which had been badly damaged by fire. It was going to cost a lot more to convert but F.N.F.C. would not allow any more, so I had to open new accounts for materials with firms such as Marley Tile and Kitchen companies When the 6 flats were finished I still owed £8,000 to various merchants.

I started to get County Court orders for these debts, I was on first names with the bailiffs. Work ground to a halt again. Nobody wanted the flats at the rear they all wanted the sea views. I got a phone call from Marley Tile. "Mr O`Brien if you don't pay the £4,000 to settle your account by noon today you will have a bankruptcy writ on your desk in the morning. Do you hear?"

"I hear. I shall put it with the rest"

A lady came to buy of one the flats at 47/48. She wanted to proceed with the sale but she owned a large property no 75 the promenade, which she would have to sell first. It was in 6 flats some rented out. She asked me if I would be interested in buying it. She was asking £11,000, which seemed more than reasonable. I said I could not at the moment but I knew some one who might be interested. I rang Ted McIlvenna the finance broker from Shaeffer House at Crosby he had mentioned a move to Southport. He bought it, moved in with his family and started to convert it into flats to sell. Mrs Hitchock, bought mine so everybody was happy with the deal. Another 6 flats were sold so I got a further advance from F.N.F.C to start on no.49.

It was taking us 6 months to do the conversion work.

But we were waiting 6 months or more in between.

I could see that the way interest was piling on and the £10,000 penalties, which Hanman had put on. I was going to have a big short fall when I had finished. I was paying interest on interest because I had not paid the original fees due.

This now must be £12 to £15 per hour 24 hours a day. It cost me £2 while I was in the toilet. Another year later I borrowed another £21,00 and completed no.50, so that was the whole block of 35 flats completed. It was now 1979. I was coming under pressure from First Fortune who had the mortgage on my house. They were going for repossession again so to appease them I put the house on the market, John Duffy of Hatch & Fielding Estate Agents, valued it at £47,5000.

Around the corner lived a old lady at 12 Oxford Road in a huge detached house in a acre of overgrown gardens. The house was wrecked! There were no gutters slates were missing from the main roof. Pigeons were flying in and out, and green moss covered the walls. In the front garden an old horse a grey roamed at will. It used to come to the front gate and if I was passing I would give him a couple of Polo mints. He had not seen a blacksmith for a long time. He had huge feet and he badly needed his hooves trimming and his mane cutting.

One Sunday afternoon I was giving the horse some mints when the old lady came down the drive.

She was in her seventies, very small, with shoulders and head slightly crouched over. She wore 2 coats and fur boots, which were unfastened. From the top of these boots the wrapping paper from a loaf of bread protruded. She obviously had her feet encased in this for extra protection. There were so many cats in the garden I could not count them. There could have been at least 30.

"Hello I see you giving my horse Barnie mints now and again. I have had him since he was born 28 years ago he is getting old now like me.

" She said in a friendly voice and smiling at me.

"He could do with a haircut," I said.

She laughed. " I know he can hardly see. Where do you live?"

"I live at 17 Westbourne Road just around the corner."

"Good heavens I lived there when I was a little girl with my mother and father, isn`t that strange, what do you do?"

"I am a builder. I renovate old property"

She seemed interested in this and said, "I have a few jobs here that need doing"

"I can see that". I said, looking at the dilapidated property.

"What is you name? She asked. "Mine is Eva Chappell, Miss".

"I am Eddie O`Brien", we shook hands through the gate, her hands were huge for the size of her little body. "I will call you Edward. Now Edward will you do little jobs for me if I call you?"

"Certainly Eva", I gave her my phone number.

Helen's mother and father came home from South Africa to live with us. Then the fun began. They argued day and night She would be shouting and screaming about things that happened 20 years before. Doors were slammed. Just what you want when you are trying to keep a roof over your head and bailiffs at your door!

You could cut the atmosphere with a knife. After a few weeks she took to her bedroom. The following weekend she went out on the Friday afternoon she had not come back by 1 am. Helen rang the police then later the hospital. There was no news of her being in any accident. She was still missing on the Saturday night and Sunday. Monday afternoon the phone rang, I answered it, "Hello Eddie it is Betty".

"And where have you been the past 3 days, we have been ringing the police and hospital worried about your safety. You could have least rung us."

"I forgot. I have been staying with my sister in law Joan. I will be back this afternoon".

"You are not coming back here you can stay were you are. Since you have been away there hasn't been any shouting, screaming, doors banging and no atmosphere."

"You can't talk to me like that, put my husband on"

I handed the phone to Jasper, he listened to her for a few moments then shouted down the phone "bollocks" and put the phone down.

"She is coming for her clothes this afternoon, she is bloody mad she has been diagnosed a manic depressive in South Africa.

She arrived at 2 p.m. with her sister-in law Joan, a lovely woman, who, over the years had visited us many time. After packing a suitcase Betty came down into the rear dining room where Joan, Jasper and myself were sitting.

She turned to me and said "Eddie O`Brien you are a evil man. I curse you until the day you die you will have no luck as long as you live."

Joan said "Betty that is dreadful thing to say"

That was the "Bent Curse" it worked very well as you will see.

At about this time I had sold a flat on The Promenade to a Jew called

Silverking. He liked the flat but wanted some extras e.g altering the kitchen extra units and waste disposal. He wanted to move some of the radiators and put in extra plugs. It amounted to £2,000 at cost.

We agreed on the price and I completed the work. He then got his surveyor around for the second time and he passed everything.

"Mr O`Brien do you mind if I just pay you for the flat now and I will pay you for the extras when I sell my bungalow in Cheadle Hulme? £2,000 was it not?"

"Yes that will be alright Mr Silverking"

Over 6 months had passed so I called to see him

" I have come for the £2000 for the extra work Mr Silverking"

I handed him an itemized bill. He went over to a cabinet and said

" Here is your bill Mr OBrien for £2,000"

"What is that for?"

"Well Mr OBrien when I came in I had to redecorate the whole flat at a cost £2,000. If you present that bill in court I will present this one."

"But you had the flat surveyed twice" He stood there with a smirk on his face.

"It's no wonder everybody hates you fucking Jews"

I never got my money. That was a typical Jewish con.

When I got home Jasper was sitting at the dining room table.

"What's the matter with you Eddie?" He asked.

"I have just been ripped off by a Jew"

"Every Jew you deal with tries to get one over on you. Mind you that`s how they are brought up. It is like in America the powerful Jewish lobby in the White House puts pressure on the American Government to send billions of dollars to the Jews in Israel so they can steal the land off the Arabs while some of their own American Blacks live in poverty.

Jasper always finishes with a joke or two.

"Eddie did you hear about the Jewish paedophile he made the kid buy his own sweets."

Mrs Cohen rang the Jewish Chronicle to put her husbands death in the paper " How much is it?"

"Up to five words £10"

" I only want to pay for two words just put 'Cohen`s dead'"

" You might have as well have five words for the same price Mrs Cohen"

"Ok put Cohen`s dead Mercedes for sale'"

" Scouse girl says to her boyfriend do you want a blow job"

" Will it effect my dole"

On the promenade there were just 12 flats left all rear ones I couldn't give them away. I even reduced the front ones to get rid of them it was a buyers market. I had sold 23 flats and had 12 left to sell. I had an investor who said he would give me £60,000 for the last 12 rear flats. He intended to rent them out. I was now dealing with a young man at F.N.F.C. called John Chennells. I rang him and asked him if I could pay him £60,000, would he let me out the stranglehold the bank had on me. He said " Yes if you can put the money on the table".

The next day I wrote to him and said that I had sent a taped recording of our telephone conversation, to my solicitor and accountant and everybody was delighted that we had a final agreement. I told him that his own words were, "Yes put the money on the table "

That made the sparks fly, F.N.F.C. Legal department wrote to me. "How dare you make a tape recording of one of our employees' conversation. Do not ever ring hear again. All correspondence in future must be in writing.

Jack Coulthurst my solicitor rang me the next day "You have certainly put the cat among the pigeons this morning Eddie. They want us to go to London next week for a sort out".

I had also mentioned in the letter about them changing the project and wanting to build new flats. Also the £ 10,000 penalties I was getting as a result their predecessors going bust. I just hope they don't want to listen to the tape because I have not got one. I had only been bluffing about that one.   The following Monday Jack and I caught the 7.40 am train at Lime Street station to Euston. We went into the 1st class and enjoyed a good breakfast. We arrived at the head office of F.N.F.C in Finsbury Pavement London for our crucial meeting at 11 a.m. I was hoping and praying that things would work out and I would get off the debt treadmill. The where a couple of solicitors and 3 bank directors their all sitting around a large oval table the walls covered in beautiful oak panelling. Their solicitor started off by giving me a roasting for taking the tape-recorded telephone conversation. " It is not the done thing in the best banking circles". Jack had told me to keep my mouth shut unless I was asked a question. Apparently the Bank had not handed over the deeds of Gai`s or the Hartleys flats at number 45.

Because if you remember I had taken money off both of them to get the work started, with the Banks permission. After hours of skilful discussion Jack hinted that it would not look good in the media if it were known a bank encouraged clients to take 'up front' money.

To then impose £10,000 penalties for 56 days extra life when the client could not pay the interest was tantamount to blackmail.

Jack had them on the back foot.

He was absolutely brilliant. He finally added, "Not to mention the Bank going insolvent causing all the problems in the first place".

The outcome was that F.N.F.C would take the £ 60,000 in full and final settlement, hand over the deeds of the 2 flats to Gai and the Hartleys. They reckoned I still owed them £90,000 and that they would right that off as well. What a relief, I am thankful that I came away with my house. I had 153 County Court Judgements Registered against me and 10 Bankruptcys put on me but I am still here!

Although free from F.N.F.C I was still in a mess. I heard about a house for sale at 4 Bank Square it was not on the market so I approached the owner a Mrs Rowan and asked her how much she wanted.

"You can have it for £10,000 it has planning for 3 flats the reason I am selling it cheap is that there is a sitting tenant in a room on the first floor a Mr Green. He says he will move if he is found a flat in that area"

"When can I view? I asked.

"We can go now if you like"

Bank Square was just off The Promenade around the corner from Agincourt. It had been a small hotel. She showed me around. It was not in such bad condition. It had 3 floors at the rear and 2 at the front.

Just as we got to the front door to leave, Mr Green came in, he was a Jew with a big nose. I explained I needed vacant possession to convert the property into flats. He assured me that he would leave if I found him a flat nearby and we shook hands on

"I will give you £10,000 Mrs Rowan if you give me 3 months to complete the sale and let me start work straight away."

She agreed. I thought it was a good buy at £10,000 and when the tenant left it would be worth a lot more. All I need now is the money. I went to see Wilf Gill, Uncle Wilf as he was known locally at the Midland Bank in Formby. "What do you want Eddie I always get a bit unnerved when you come in?"

I told him about the property but did not mention the tenant "

I only need £1,000 for the deposit and £5,000 working capital then completion in 3 months"

He agreed, so we started the work the week after. It was essential Mr Green, the tenant, kept his word and moved out .

He also had his wife with him. Their room was filthy. She was filthy the smell was awful. I started to look around for a flat and found one in the next road Booth Street. I gave him the Landlords' address and phone number and he said that he would go and see it.

The rent was only £2 more but it had 3 rooms. I saw him a week later and he said his wife did not like it. Over the next 3 months I found 4 more flats Mrs Green did not like. Work was progressing quickly.

He was now in the way because all the copper piping and wiring had to pass through his room to the top floor flat. I asked him the next day what was going on. "I have spent time and effort looking for 4 flats for you and you won't take them, you are bringing the work to a halt."

"Mr Obrien, I am not leaving until you pay me £1,000. I know I am stopping the job and you can't finish with me still here." This was where his Jewish education came to the fore

"Mr Green you agreed to leave, I have found you 4 flats. I have stuck to our agreement, you are getting nothing you devious Jewish bastard but you are leaving, have no doubt about that"

During the day his filthy wife used to bring old men back for sexual services some were so old they could hardly climb the stairs.

One old chap knocked on her door and said, "Are you doing business?" She said" yes"

"I have only got a pound"

"That's all right I have got change"

The next morning my joiner Frank lifted the floor boards and punched a hole in their ceiling and poured a dry bag of thistle plaster over both of them as they lay in bed. They looked like 2 ghosts covered in powder.

"That's for starters, you are not putting us lads out of work, you Jewish twat." Frank screamed through the hole in the ceiling.

When we were having our tea break, tempers were rising.

Some of the lads wanted to go and throw him out into the street. Harry the plumber said, "It's no wonder a Jew cannot join a golf club in the U.K."

Jack the plasterer said, " During the War in Berlin there were 10,000 Jews men women and children in hiding from the Germans who wanted to gas them but they could not find them. The Germans offered rewards to any one who could locate them. There were Jews called Geiffers. They betrayed thousands of their fellow Jews even babies for rewards and they were gassed. Don`t forget the Jews hanged unarmed British prisoners of war in 1948.

We bricked Mr Green's windows up but still he would not go. He was shouting through the door I want a £1000. I found out he was working at a penny arcade on Neville Street in the afternoons and evenings.

We put all his belongings in bin bags, none of the furniture was his.

I paid a months' rent for a flat in Victoria Street owned by a women called Black Annie.

We put his goods in there then I went around to the arcade.

"Mr Green you have just moved. Here are your keys to 8 Victoria Street. I have paid a months rent for you."

"I am not moving " he argued.

"That's what you think. You have just moved"

He then said, "but, don't I get any money?"

"Here's a 'tenner'," I said calling the other arcade assistant, who I knew as "Creosote Lol". But that's another story. I wanted him to witness this. Mr Green accepted my kind offer and I left.

The lads and I went to the London pub to celebrate. An hour later the 'phone rang. It was my wife Helen. It appeared that Southport Police had rung and wanted to know why I had evicted Mr& Mrs Green.

I was requested to present myself at the police station forthwith.

I went and explained the situation and how I had paid a months rent for a flat etc. and Mr Green accepted my financial inducement in front of a witness. "Can you prove this?" asked the policeman.

"I certainly can. It was witnessed by 'Creosote Lol" a fellow worker of Mr Green's at the arcade. I heard nothing more of the incident. A couple of months later we finished the jobs. I sold the 2 front flats but could not get rid of the rear flat where the profit was. But at least while I was working I had cash flow.

I got a 'cut off' notice from the Gas Board. They were coming the next day. I managed to borrow some money from a pal and paid the bill the next morning first thing, I rang the Gas Board to inform them that I had paid but they said that the man had already left and if I showed him the receipt he would not cut us off. He had not arrived by 1 p.m. I had to go out so I asked Jasper who was still with us, if he would show the receipt to the gasman when he came. "I have put the receipt on the mantelpeice in the front lounge,. Jasper alright "

I came back at 2 p.m. there was a police car outside. 2 policemen were at the door with Jasper and the gasman. The gasman was a little ginger haired bastard from Kirkby. He had cut us off a few times before.

He definitely had the 'Liverpool Chip'! He sees a big house he sees wealth he thinks. He thinks like some scouser`s do "I have nottin no one gives us nottin" I will cut this rich bastard's gas off come what may. It's them or us.

One of the policemen asked if I was the owner.

"Yes, officer what is the problem"?

" The gasman says that your father-in-law assaulted him. He alleges that he was thrown out of the house as he was going about his lawful business, which was cutting your gas supply off because you had not paid the bill"

"You mean this 72 year old pensioner assaulted this gentleman and threw him out of the house? For your information officer, the gas bill has been paid we have a receipt to prove it.". I turned to my father-in-law. "What happened Jasper?"

"Well this bastard gasman called 20 minutes ago to cut us off, I said that we had paid but I could not find the receipt. I told that you would be back at 2p.m. and asked him in to have a cup of tea. I said that you would show him the receipt.

But he said, 'No. I'm coming in to cut you off.' He just pushed past me and as you know nobody can come in .without a warrant. I jumped on his back and decked him in the hall and slung him out. By the time he came back with the police I had found the receipt, it had fallen behind the armchair."

"Is that correct officer this bully who attacked a old aged pensioner needed a warrant to enter my house?"

" That is correct sir " said the policemen as they walked away.

"You did very well there Jasper for a old scouse sea dog".

Jasper said the 'Liverpool Chip' was well known all over the U.k. some Scousers are always moaning about working conditions wanting a '30 hour' week and £5 more than the boss. He said not all scousers have this socialist philosophy.

"I should have made him a Landowner a good kick in the balls would have given him 2 acres"

He reckoned it held back big investment for Liverpool and Manchester would leave us behind in the future. He had to throw a joke in. "

This Scouser is walking along Southport Promenade with his family.

One of his lads has a tin bucket and spade, as they pass this gleaming Rolls Royce he scratches the Rolls Royce from end to end.

He cracks the kid across the head " What have I told you will break that bloody spade."

A few days later we had a gentleman call he said he had heard the house might be put on the market as he would be interested. He came to view the next day. When I opened the front door he just filled it.

He was huge6feet 7 inches about 25 stone baldhead horned rimmed glasses. I showed him around and he was impressed. He wanted to open a Rest Home. He already had 2 in Birkdale and he offered me the full asking price of £47,500. He asked me if he could have people from the

Health Department and Social Service come around to inspect it.

He came back a week later. It was bad news. The Town Planning would not give him permission for a Rest Home. He was full of apologies and very disappointed. He asked me what line of business I was in then he said would like Helen and me to go out for a meal with him and his wife also called Helen. He picked us up at 8p.m. in his Jaguar and we went to the Bold Hotel on Lord Street. We had a few drinks and a lovely meal then went into the bar. Both wives were getting on well chatting away. He wanted to open a string of Rest Homes then open a Business Agency buying and selling them.

"Eddie if you see any suitable properties let me know and I will pay you a commission on them"

"I will if I see any suitable properties Malcolm, are you busy at the moment?" I said.

"I have two Rest Homes, my wife runs at the moment. She is a SRN and I have sold 5 others. I pick them up relatively cheap, give them a coat of paint put new carpets in and they sell like hot cakes, and they are always full when I sell them." He started to laugh.

"You see Eddie, don't breath a word of this to anyone. I buy these Rest Homes, which are usually run down, with 5 or 6 patients in. After I have tarted them up I advertise them in Dalton's Weekly. The potential buyer comes along and on that day I bring a coach load of patients from the 2 Rest Homes I own. I tell them they are going out to lunch and fill the place with 35 patients on £140 per week.

They can`t wait to sign the contract which they must sign that day. After they have left I take my patients back with me leaving the original 5 or 6 patients in. It is quite legal because patients can move anytime they want. They are not fixtures and fitting I made a £100,000 on one Do you know Eddie my parents were in the Iron and Steel Business. My Mother did the Ironing and my Father did the Stealing.

He dropped us back at home about midnight I thanked him for meal.

Eva the nice little old lady from Oxford Road with all the animals rang. Could I come and fix her water main, it had burst. I took Jasper with me because I am useless at D.I.Y. She met us at the gate and took us around the back down into the cellar. Jasper soon had the old lead pipe fixed with a bit of solder it had been patched up many times before.

"Who is this gentleman, is he one of your men?"

"No Eva this is Jasper my father-in-law, the best plumber in Europe he put the central heating in at Buckingham Palace"

"Did he really? How much do I owe you? Well I can't pay you until I get

my pension next week. All my money goes on the cats and dogs you ".
"Don't worry Eva there is no charge. It has only taken a minute.
How many animals have you got to look after Eva?"
"At the last count there were 26 cats and 25 dogs, the cats are naughty
they keep having kittens I will have to get them on the pill"
She put her hand to her mouth and giggled like a little schoolgirl.
As we walked back down the drive another old lady was waving out of
the ground floor front window. Next to her was a big Airedale its paws
up on the window ledge.
"That's my tenant Miss Jane Pedley she has the ground floor. I have the
first floor, don't have a cup of tea off her, she does not wash her cups"
A few days later we went to fix the washer on Eva`s tap, I knocked on
her front door, all the dogs started barking at once it was bedlam.
"You go into the lounge. I will get the dogs out of the kitchen."
It was like going back in time there were cobwebs hanging from the
ceiling, thick dust everywhere. The curtains were falling to pieces you
could not see out of the windows. There were stacks of newspapers
some with Churchill on the front, old ration books, soot had fallen down
the chimney and was piled in the hearth.
"Excuse the mess Edward, I sacked the maid in 1957 she was picking her
nose while she was peeling the potatoes. I won't have that. I tried to
replace her, in fact I might put a advert in the paper this week, I might
just be lucky"
We went through into the kitchen there were dirty pots and pans, dishes
of stale food, dozens of bottles of milk going green and mice running
across the shelves. Eva went into the other room.
Jasper said, " let's get out of here quick before we catch something."
He had the washer on in no time!
He said, "This is another one of those houses where you have to wipe
your feet on the way out"
Eva popped her head around the door " Would you like a cup of tea
gentlemen?"
We both said at the same time " No thanks Eva".
A couple of days later Jane rang up from the ground floor,
Could I fix her electric fire as it was the only means of heat?
Jane opened the door. She was in her 'seventies' walking with the aid of
2 sticks. Her hair was swept back in to a bun, rather ugly, big horsy teeth
and bright red lipstick put on with a trowel, but she seemed pleasant
enough. The fire was very old and had a single wire running through.
Even I had no trouble fixing it. Jane`s flat was not as bad as Eva`s you

could see the floor in parts.

"You are Edward I take it. Eva has told me a lot about you and that you now live in her old house. Her family were very wealthy but not as wealthy as mine. My father was a major shareholder in Midland Railways before they were nationalised." She paused for a while and then continued. "When Eva was growing up she used to invite all her friends around for a game of croquet on the front lawn. Only the best people were invited, she had horses and a riding school at the rear. She would take her pupils along the beach to Ainsdale. She did love her horses.

She got engaged to a young local doctor and he wanted to get rid of the smelly horses but she refused so he gave her a ultimatum

" It`s me or the horses" he never stood a chance.

The big Airedale came bounding over jumped up with his feet on my chest.

"This is Harold, Edward my best friend here sit down for a minute, would you like a cup of tea?"

"No thank you Jane" I had remembered what Eva had said but she had no room to talk. There were 3 mice lying on the top of the pelmet and 3 or 4 running around the room, there was a half eaten cheese sandwich on the settee beside Jane,

" Come on boys ",   She started to throw bits of cheese and bread crumbs to the mice, the 3 mice from of the top of the pelmet absailed down and 2 of them ran along the back of the settee and Jane was feeding them out of her hand.

"Are`nt they lovely, that's Willie, Geoffrey and Ivan, I have names for most of them"

There was about 10 mice running around I felt a bit uncomfortable,.
I am not afraid I of mice, but you don't want them sitting on your knee, I shuffled feet and they scattered.

"Do you know Edward Eva is very eccentric I remember when her mother died about 30 years ago, it was on a Tuesday afternoon. Eva was holding the stepladder for the maid who was dusting the top of the curtains, Eva`s mother who was 90 years old was sitting in the armchair facing the door, the maid looked down and said to Eva, "I think your mothers dead". Eva went over to her mother and said "I think you are right I will ring the doctor"

About 10 minutes after the door bell goes Eva opens the door it is not the doctor it is the gas man to read the meter, he is standing in the hall way facing Eva's mother.

"Good morning Mrs Chappell"

Eva said "It is no good talking to her she is dead"

" She is a character".

"That fire is working alright now. Just ring if you need help Jane. Cherio" I stepped over Harold who was fast asleep on the carpet with a mouse next to him. Eva rang me again a few days later she seemed upset she asked me to come around as it was urgent. When Eva opened the door I could see she had been crying,

"Come in Edward, I have had some terrible news the bank said they are going to take the house off me if I don't pay the money back that I owe them, could you help me I am at my wits end with worry, what will happen to the animals can you help financially?".

"I am afraid not Eva I am in the same boat myself, I have had to put my house up for sale for the same reason you could not have asked at a worst time, which bank is it?

"It is the Natwest I only owe £6,000"

"But the house is worth a lot more than £ 6,000".

"I know that Edward if it was empty but I have a sitting tenant, and I don't want to leave here after all these years I want to die here like my mother and father I don't know anyone else who would help, friends are thin on the ground when you need help".

I stayed with her trying to comfort her, "It will take the bank months to get you to court Eva I am sure something will turn up, don't give up yet". That night I could not get to sleep thinking about poor Eva, there must be something I could think of I had got through many scrapes myself. The next morning it came to me,.

Wilf Gill   the best bank manager in the world. As soon as the bank opened, I rang and he said he would talk to Eva but was not promising anything but he would discuss it, I made a appointment the next day for 11 a.m. I dashed around to tell Eva the good news, she was delighted and giggling and laughing like an excited child.

"It is not 100% certain that he will give you the money but I don't think he would see you if he was not going to. I will call for you at 10.40a.m. tomorrow morning Eva so put your Sunday best on"

I called for as arranged she looked a sight, she had a riding outfit on those old fashioned jodhpurs and old coat with egg stains and covered in dog hairs on her head was a south American Gaucho hat.

"I cant fasten my boots Edward as my feet are swollen the bread paper stops them chaffing"

"Don't worry Eva, you look great".

She dragged her feet along the floor, I opened the door for her when she had got in she said "I feel excited Edward."

We arrived at the bank in Chappel Lane just before 11 A.M. A good omen I thought with Eva`s surname being the same. The bank was very busy, everyone seemed to turn around and look at Eva, she just smiled, I went to the counter

"I have a appointment at 11a.m. with Mr Gill it is Miss Chappell and OBrien. A few minutes later Wilf opened the door, his mouth fell open he whispered, "Were do you find them?"

I told her on the way down not to mention that she had a sitting tenant banks don't like them. He asked me about the house I said it could with a bit of money spent on it and it was in an acre of land, he was well covered for the loan Eva wanted and it was freehold.

He lent her £8,000 she was delighted. When we arrived back at her house she said "Oh Edward you are my saviour, come up we will have a glass of sherry to celebrate my good fortune"

We went up to her lounge she took her riding gear off went over to a large ornate cocktail cabinet with beautiful glass doors. She reached inside and she held 2 glasses in one hand she turned away slightly and blew all the dust out of them making her cough, she reached in again brought out the sherry bottle cobwebs trailing behind it.

"Here Edward " she handed me a glass of sherry there was dust particles floating on the top, she raised her glass." To a very good day you have saved my home and I will never forget you Edward as long as I live".

She downed her drink in one, I just pretended to take a sip.

"Would you like another one Edward?".

" No thanks Eva I am driving, you have another one yourself".

She went and poured herself another sherry I threw mine into the soot on the hearth.

"Come and sit with me on the settee"

I sat next to her, hope she does not get a grip of me, she put her glass on the coffee table now "Edward hold my hands," her hands were nearly as big as mine. "You are a big strong man I want all your strength to transfer to my old frail body " She closed her eyes, and we held hands for 5 minutes.

"I feel much better now, I have some photographs of your house when I lived there, I will show them to you"

She got a shoebox out of the sideboard. "There is the tennis court at the back and there is the front garden in full blossom, that is my mother and father by the rose bush, my dog Shep is lying at there feet he was a lovely dog."

"Who is that Eva? I pointed to a photo in the shoebox.

"That was me when I was eighteen".

She handed me the photo, she looked so beautiful, like a young
Elizabeth Taylor, I bet all the young men were chasing you Eva".

"One or two" she put her hand to her mouth and giggled, we used to
play Postman`s Knock but only with boys we new very well" "
You little devil Eva"

" Do you know what Edward, there another favour you can do for me"
"What is that Eva"?

"When I die Edward will you cut my wrists for me?"

"Certainly Eva if that is what you want, but why is that?

"Well my mother was terrified of being buried alive I have visions of her
scratching at the coffin lid.

"What would you mother say if she was alive today?"

"Let me out"

We seemed to get our wires crossed, unless it was the sherry.

"Eva when you die do you want to be buried or cremated?""

"Surprise me Edward".

"I have to go now Eva, ring me if you want anything"

There was no reply she had fallen asleep I put her coat over her and
slipped out.

I was having a pint in the London, went to the gents and a man came in
who used to be a tenant of mine Bill O`Neill

".Hello Eddie are you still buying property?

"Have not bought much lately Bill".

I have a house for sale at 45 Hall Street just around the corner it is in
good condition I have just done it up ".

"How much?" "£13000,I have the keys here go and have a look".

I went and had a look it was a bargain alright, I went back to the pub,
"Why are you selling it so cheap Bill?".

"I have a contract on to work abroad. In a couple of weeks"

"O.k Bill it a deal "I gave him my solicitors details.

"Just one thing Eddie I need a deposit off you for £250 and it is your`s

"If I give you a deposit I want to put a tenant in and I keep the keys "

I gave him the £250 the next day and kept the keys, my idea was to put
Helens auntie and uncle Mr & Mrs Dewhurst in there as they elderly and
were having trouble climbing the stairs at 21 Leicester Street where they
had moved. They were delighted with the house when they moved in.
I would have a few months to find the purchase money.

A couple of months went by no contract off O`Neill for 45 Hall Street it did not bother me because I was getting the rent A couple of weeks later Helens aunt &uncle had a visitor from the Abbey National Building Society wanting to know what they were doing in a house that had been repossessed from a Mr O"Neill .

"Mr O`Brien is the landlord" explained Mrs Dewhurst.

"And who is Mr O`Brien we have never heard of him" replied the Abbey National Manager. The next week they got a court order for eviction .

I said I would go on their behalf and explain to the court what had happened. The morning of the hearing at Southport County Court I arrived at 9.45 AM the first hearing is at 10 am the court usher had put a couple of names on the board. I was glad to see I was first in Dewhurst v Stone solicitors. When we got into the courtroom the recorder Sat the end of the table the solicitor and myself either side.

The solicitor started of he wanted damages, interest and compensation off Mr Dewhurst he went on for about 20 minutes I was not paying much attention I just wanted to explain things.

The Recorder said "Now Mr Dewhurst what have you to say for yourelf?."

"I am not Mr Dewhurst they are a elderly couple and I am representing them"

"Right then carry on"

"I bought the house in good faith"

"What house?"

"45 Hall Street "

"What are you talking about, this is a car accident claim, nothing to do with a house, you are in the wrong court, get out you have thrown, the whole days schedule out."

I made a quick exit, when I got outside I looked up at the notice board and saw that Dewhurst v Abbey National was 11:30A.M. which was not up when I first came in. I went back in at 11:30 a.m. the atmosphere was icy to say the least, he gave the Building Society possession.

I found a place was found in a rest home for Mr & Mrs Dewhurst where they would be better off.

First Fortune had obtained a eviction order on our house we had 10 weeks to get out. I put the house up for sale with Hatch & Feilding at £47,500 A month went by there was no sign of any buyers.

Eva rang she was in trouble again she had some large vet bills and had being buying cat and dog food by the van load.

"Edward do you think that nice man at the bank will help me again?

"I don't think so Eva, have you paid any money into the bank?"

"I can't feed the animals and pay money into the bank as well can I Edward"

"I think I might have the solution Eva. What if I was to buy the derelict Coach House off you at the rear I could do it up I would have a home and you would have some money, what do you think?"

"I don't know Edward no one has lived in there for 50 years it is falling down"

"You think about it Eva and I will call around tomorrow"

I called the next day, she said I could have it for £6,000 but no land she needed all the land to exercise her dogs I agreed and told her to go and see her solicitor. She rang me again a few days later asked me to call around she had bad news. "Come in Edward" we went into the lounge there were 5 dogs on the settee.

"These are my own dogs pointing to 3 lassie collies that's Rusty, Dusty and Musty pointing to 2 poodles one black and one white that's Chalkie and Nigger , the black one is nigger."

"How did you get on at your solicitors?"

"He advised me not to sell to you because there would be disputes over right of way and splitting the deeds etc."

"There should not be if it is done properly, I have another solution what if I bought your house as well and rented this house and all the land to you for £1 per year how would that do?

That sounds fantastic Edward, how much are you going to give me?"

"You will have to go and see your solicitor again and sort something out with him"

She rang me again a couple of days later "Hello Edward is £18,000 alright?

"That's fine with me send me a contract"

"I am very happy Edward you have saved my life again."

Hatch and Feilding the estate agent rang to say some one wanted to view our house. A Chinese family came there was about 15 of them, they made a offer of £45,000 I accepted on the agreement that we had a 2 month completion being under pressure from First Fortune they agreed. But I needed to have the coach house ready before the sale went through .I made a appointment to see Wilf Gill at Formby the following afternoon.

I always go in the afternoon. "Good afternoon Wilf"

"Not you again Eddie, I thought you had gone to the wall"

"Only a rumour Wilf, do you know that lovely old lady I brought in last time Miss Chappel.

"You mean the lovely old lady I lent £8,000 who is overdrawn and has not paid a penny back yet"

"Well, Wilf I can help you clear her overdraft, in fact we can help each other, I have a buyer for my house at £45,000 I owe about £15,000 if I get my solicitor to give you a undertaking to pay the proceeds in here that £30,000. I want to buy Miss Chappell's house and the Coach house at the rear for £18,000 which will clear her debt don't forget you have £,8000 out on it already ,then I need £30,000 to renovate it you will have 2 properties as security for £48,000"

"O.K Eddie you are on but I don't want you overdrawn, or me chasing you around the bank like last year".

He was referring to a incident last year, I was well overdrawn and he took my cheque book off me so I could not write anymore cheques out, on the way out I went to the counter got another one.

The next day Friday I went in at lunch time when I thought he would on his lunch hour I drew £400 in cash, as I looked up I saw him behind the counter he spotted me so I made a run for the door, he started to run behind the counter we were neck and neck then a women blocked my path with a pram which slowed me a little, he caught me at the door and grabbed the money off me.

" Good try Eddie but not good enough"

I had about 6 men working all hours to get the Coach House ready in time. We made the downstairs stable which housed the coach and horses into a huge lounge 20ft x40 ft and had built a huge stone fireplace, open beams on the ground floor and the original black cast iron range in the dining room and beautiful Elizabeth Anne kitchen with stable doors at the rear.

The Coach House was ready to move into and it was completion day on our house it was approaching lunchtime and Jack my solicitor rang to say he was getting no response from the buyer's solicitors.

He was concerned because the house would be repossessed at 4 p.m. if they failed to complete that would ruin everything.

I rang the Chinese gentleman at home, they said he was out this was at 1 pm, no return call so I rang back at 2p,m. they said he was still out, 2 hours to go I rang at 2.30P.M. Still out. My solicitor rang me at 3p.m. the buyers solicitor had been on and said his client was now only willing to pay £42,000 not £45,000, I had shown my hand by ringing him desperate to complete, I had no choice but drop £3000 we completed just in time.

We moved into the Coach House it was really idyllic a lovely setting back from the road and surrounded by trees.

Eva would come up the drive to take the dogs in the paddock, she would have 5 dogs on leads in each hand and about 10 cats following behind. As I would pass her house at the bottom of the drive she would ask me to get her shopping from the village or her pension .

I think she was glad we had moved in. We still had our hand holding sessions, which she said, revitalized her

We invited Eva and Jane in for a Christmas drink separately they were great friend but could not stand each other They thought the house was wonderful.

Helen`s sister Sheila and her husband Pete came on New Year Eve we were having a good booze up when the phone rang at 12;30 am it was Jane she was sobbing her heart out. Harold had dropped dead on the carpet could I come down, Pete came with me, Harold was dead on the floor I asked Jane what had happened she said Harold had been mousing, now and again he would have a mad half hour chasing the mice one had stuck in his throat. Jane was leaning on her two sticks tears cascading down her cheeks. "We had better put him outside Jane and we will come and bury him in the morning."

" No, No it is to cold for him, carry him into the bedroom".

They were 3 mice on top of the pelmet looking down I am sure they were smiling. We carried Harold through into the bedroom, it was a very large room, it had twin beds and a huge wardrobe with cobwebs sweeping across to the dressing table, the only lighting was a standard lamp in the corner it looked like a setting for a horror movie.

"Put him on the other bed Edward put his head on the pillow put that blanket over him it is going to be a cold night."

We went back into the lounge Jane was till crying, the only heating was a single bar electric fire.

"Would you like a brandy Jane?"

"Yes please Edward" I nipped up to the house and brought a large brandy back for Jane, after half an hour she seemed more relaxed.

You go to bed now Jane and we will come and see you in the morning, not a good time to wish her a happy New Year. Next morning I got the wheelbarrow out and my 3 sons, Eddie who went into the paddock to dig the grave Mark and Steven an myself went around to Jane`s ,she started to weep ,I took the wheelbarrow into the bedroom ,we put Harold in it he filled it completely.

"Could you put his rubber duck in as well Edward?"

She handed me the rubber duck and I placed it in next to Harold, then

we set off around to the paddock, Jane following slowly behind.
Eddie had dug the grave so I tipped Harold in, but the grave was not deep enough his feet were sticking up in the air, it was wide enough so I thought I would turn Harold on his side, I pushed the spade under his body to turn him over, as I did I caught the rubber duck which squawked and we all jumped back with fright,

We realized what had happened we roared laughing, Jane had just come into the paddock we managed to control ourselves. After the funeral, I took her in and made her a cup of tea and stayed with her for a while. Helen decided she wanted a horse Eva said she could put it in the paddock. We went to see a horse called Charlie Girl it was being sold by a lady called Jean Walsh at Tarleton. Helen explained she was only a novice rider and wanted a quite horse suitable, Helen was told that this horse was ideal for a novice. We paid £1000 for it, but Jean Walsh forget to tell Helen that the horse reared the most dangerous thing a horse can do, if it stands up on its back legs then falls back on top of the rider the rider is dead.

Ginger McCain, Red Rums trainer was only about half a mile away and the stable lads used to ride past our house every morning on the way to the beach, I went out one morning and explained about the horse rearing and Helen could not ride it, one of the stable lads said he would sort it out. About 5 of them tied their racehorses to our fence and came into the paddock. Charlie Girl who according to Jean Walsh was a novice ride was saddled up and brought in one of the stable boys mounted and gingerly walked her around the paddock before mounting her.

Next thing Charlie Girl rears it is standing up straight on its hind legs you could see the terror in the rider eyes, was he going to die was the horse going to fall back on top of him, could he jump clear, Jean Walsh new this could happen to a human being but she still took the money.

The horse fell backward everybody screamed miraculously the rider fell clear he was a very lucky boy. The stable lads could not believe some evil person had sold it to a novice rider, they never came back.

I wanted to take the horse back and get our money back but Helen wanted to keep it as she had got attached to it.

About a year later in the spring of 1981,I was concerned about Eva`s health, she was not going to bed and sleeping in the chair she was not eating properly living on tea and biscuit she was so independent and did not like interference Eva rang me in the afternoon to see if I would get her pension but she said " I will have to ring off now Edward I have had a deluge from the rear".

I called her friend Jane Lowe who worked with the R.S.P.C A she came
around to see Eva and called the doctor, a few days later Eva was back
on her feet looking after the animals she looked very frail, her shoulders
stooping lower.

The following week Jane wrang up from the ground floor flat she was
having a nosebleed and it would not stop, I went to her she was sitting in
the armchair, there was blood all down the front of her dress.

"How long had it been like this Jane?"

" About 20 minutes it just wont stop ". I got a cold wet towel and put it
on the back of her neck then I put her head back put it just got worst.

"I had better call the doctor Jane"

" No doctor, no doctor Edward"

I waited a few more minutes and called the ambulance, I went with her
to Southport Promenade Hospital After waiting for over an hour the
nurse said they were keeping her in as she had lost so much blood.

I rang back later in the evening, she was comfortable and they would let
her come home at lunchtime tomorrow. The next day I went to pick her
up she was in bed I hardly recognized her, she was clean with her hair
combed and the nurses had put lipstick on her she had scrubbed up well.

I sat in the waiting room while she dressed, a nurse came over and said "
Is that your mother?" " No it is a neighbour .

"Good I was going to tell you off, do you now we had to wash her feet
with vim and throw her clothes in the bin, we could not get a comb
through her hair"

"As I said I am just a neighbour, I am just helping her I don't need a
lecture."

Unfortunately, Eva was not so lucky she was admitted to hospital, I went
in to see her early afternoon she looked like a skeleton, in fact I thought
she was dead. I was stopped in my tracks by the site of her, the women
in the next bed said "She is only asleep, wake her up"

"No she needs the sleep I will come back this evening"

I came back in the evening, Eva was propped up with the pillows she
gave me a lovely smile, "Pull that chair up Edward right next to my bed,
now hold my hands and let that young strength of your young body
come through into my body, it will get me through the night."

I went each evening for the next 5 nights. Helen never came ,I was
sitting by her bed, just holding her hands.

"You know Edward I am dying I have had a wonderful life with my horses
and dogs and am on my last ride now, you have been a good friend to
me Edward, you helped me in my hour of need, you have all your life

before you take it by the scruff of the neck, so this is goodbye Edward ".
"Good bye Eva". She squeezed my hand and drifted off to sleep, my eyes
were filling up I was biting my lip I had to get out.

Eva died that night she was buried at Birkdale Cemetery with her mother
and father. The R.S.P.C.A took all the animals away the place did not
seem the same without her.

Jane was not happy in that big house on her own she had lost Harold
and now Eva she felt lonely and isolated and with dogs and cats gone
there seemed more mice than ever, not that she would mind.

About 3 months later Jane was getting really depressed the flat was
getting worse half eaten meals left on the table and in the kitchen, dirty
pots and pans flies everywhere. I suggested to her that if I could find a
flat in a nice area were there were other people she could talk to be and
be neighbourly with would she like to move.

"I would be delighted, I would move tomorrow". I found a nice ground
floor flat near Hesketh Park she was very pleased Jane moved in was a
lot happier having neighbours to talk to.

A local architect Bill Lowe suggested putting planning permission in to
see what could be built on our land .

They gave us planning for 3 detached or a block of 12 flats, next door no
14 was also in 2 flats with tenants in standing in a acre of land I thought
both together would make a wonderful site. I found out who owned it
and bought for £36,000 with the tenants in then I gave them an
inducement to leave, which they gladly accepted.

I then put in planning for 14 detached houses, which was in keeping with
the area. It was turned down. In 1985 I sold the land to a Life Insurance
Company, for £220,000 they put in planning for 21 houses and guess
what it sailed through, isn't that strange. If I had been a Freemason
I would have got the planning.

With selling the land we had no where for the horse so we had to move
my mate Bernard found a place in Formby just a few miles away, it was
called Rose Stud Farm, it had 19 acres and a stable block but only a small
prefab to live in.

Unfortunately somebody jumped in before us and bought it. Across the
road on the corner of Broad Lane there was empty house called Warren
House in 2 acres of land but along side there were about 20 gypsy
caravans. Shortly after it came up for sale at £33,000 nobody else was
interested, I wonder why. I bought it thought it was a bargain, the coach
house fetched £80,000. I had turned things around in the black at last,
I still had a lot of debts to clear I felt a big weight off my shoulders. The

house was a wreck the gypsies had stripped all the all the plumbing out we had too practically rebuild it.

Most of the gypsies were Irish so with my name being O`Brien we got on a treat the generators were noisy but we got used to it.

We had been in about a week, Helen was looking out of the front window, "Look at all that land the house has got across the road".

"Let us get unpacked first before we look at anything else"

I built a stable block for 6 horses thinking we could rent some out.

As we passed the stood farm we could see a horse in the field it was jet black but it looked like a skeleton all its ribs were showing we found out it had been abandoned and the girl who owned it had left owing stable rent. It had been a race horse brought over from Ireland to aim for the grand national and at one time it had been trained by Ginger McCain but it had injured it leg and could not race, to cut a long story short we adopted it, and put it in the stable next to Charlie Girl and they got on great. After six months Helen had it in great shape, She then decided that seeing Charlie Girl was unsafe to ride she would put her in foal she sent her away to be covered by a Irish Draft Stallion.

In the house across the road lived a old couple Mr & Mrs Farrington they rented out kennels for the dogs used for hare coursing at nearby Altcar so the Animal Rights group used to smash there windows and kick there front door in give them a hard time. I asked them if they ever thought of selling I would be very interested in buying.

Soon Charlie Girls foal was due anytime now, I went for a pint, since Helen got interested in the horsy world with the green wellie women she did not want to go out with me she hardly left the place unless to go to a horse show. I came home about 11:30 p.m. no one in the house so I went out to the stables Helen and her friend Christine were leaning over the stable door Charlie Girl was lying down you could see the foals head sticking out, but Charlie Girl was to close to the wall the foals head was nearly touching it, the mother was getting frantic kicking her legs out in frustration.

I opened the door and went in, I stroked her head and neck to try and calm her down but she was still lashing out I went to the other end, it was her first foal so she probably did not know what to do either.

"Come on Charlie you will be alright" she looked me straight in the eye, she new I was trying to help her, if I could push her over she would be away from the wall but I could not get near enough.

Her rear foot just missed my head I moved in quick and gently eased the foal out there was blood and afterbirth all over my trousers it was a good job I had had a pint or two.

The foal was lying down, Charlie heaved herself on to her feet and went over to the foal and started to lick her in 5 minutes it was up on its feet I was surprised to see how big it was whilst I was patting Charlie`s neck she turned and give my face a big lick, as much to say thank you.

Not a bad nights work for a butcher I was very pleased with myself.

The old chap over the road died and a few months after his widow Mrs Farrington came over asked us if we wanted to buy her house she did not feel safe on her own .

The house was called Fernilea it had bad settlement in the left hand front corner it must have dropped nearly a foot the front bedroom had a very sharp incline, we paid £70,000 for it had to start all over again getting it renovated there was no gas so we installed oil central heating no sewer mains so we used a septic tank. The house had a good feel about it felt a friendly house the windows in the front went down nearly to the floor, there was a stream at the front crossed by a small bridge the cars had to go around the rear.

We had 2 rottweilers Elsa and Kimber supposed to be guard dogs they did not even bark, let any one in then licked them, we also had a Alsatian called Sheba she was a better guard dog.

Next was a baby goat called Oliver who would run around with the dogs then wanted to come in the house when they came in.

The were a row of pigsties at the back of the house so I converted them into 8 stables.

I got £77,000 for the house over the road Warren House

I sold it to another builder I new called Roy he moved in with his girl friend Vera she had 2 daughters and a son. They changed the stables into a boarding kennels for dogs which I had plans to do also but instead of treading on their toes .

I built a cattery for 20 cats and called it Aristocat .We put in double glazing central heating pictures and plants also rugs on the floor it was like home from home for the cats, they had there own chalet with a bedroom on the wall with a ladder running up to it and of course soft music they favoured radio 2. Helen was soon turning people away they were quite surprised when they came in, so I built another one which would take 80 cats it was built like a huge bungalow 80 ft x40 ft .

I got prices of different trades men and soon had it finished my joiner Terry made and fitted all the cat chalets. We borrowed £90,000 of the Natwest Bank Helen went with me as all the properties were in joint names But she opened the Aristocat bank account her name only,

£90,000 overdraft in joint named account That meant the income from the Cattery would go in her account and the interest and charges would build up on the joint account.

The cattery was ready for the summer of 1991. The small cattery took 20 cats the new cattery would take 80 cats, it was split into 4 sections each taking 20 cats but Helen only wanted 60 cats leaving one section empty. I pointed out we would lose 20 cats at £3;50 per cat £70 per day, she said 80 cats was enough to look after, I thought if you were looking after 80 cats another 20 would not make much difference, 80 cats a day at £3,50 £ 240 per day , £1680 per week not every week

She now charges £7   Did she have something up her sleeve I did not know about for the future?.   The cattery was busy at holiday time Christmas, Easter the summer holidays.

Helen hired a lady to run the cattery she was to busy with her horses.

I found some properties at Sandbrook Way Woodvale just outside of Southport they consisted of a block of shops with flats above I planned to renovate the flats and covert the shops into flats.

There were 5 shops and 5 flats so I bought the block except one flat, which was separately owned I sold no 33 /21 to my son Steven he sold the flat above and got the shop for nothing, he then opened video shop which was doing quite well, but being a fat lazy bastard he put people in to work instead of himself who robbed him, He then opens another video shop around the corner in Heathfield Road against my advice it had closed down once, he closed them both in the end, there was one amusing incident in the shop a old lady came in on a zimmer well into her seventies. "Blue Movies son"

"We are not allowed to stock them love "

" No do you want to buy some?"

At this time the housing market was buoyant you could say booming. Banks were lending money I joined the Yorkshire Bank and the Bank of Scotland, in for a penny in for a pound, I never had any trouble borrowing money only paying it back. I was offered another six cheap houses in Southport so I bought them as well. It took me about 10 months to get these properties ready for the market then interest rates went up mortgage rates went to the highest ever and the boom was over. I had 13 properties on my hands not a buyer in sight in the mire again, but it is no good moaning that's the chance you take it is the rub of the green.

All the Banks were screaming for their money back. I got myself into this mess, it is down to me no one else so it is down to me to get myself out.

Everything was at stake including the house and cattery at Formby .
I was into various Banks for about half a million pounds, it was shit or
bust. So I decided to sell some of the properties to my sons Mark bought
a couple and Eddie, Steven bought three or four but he charged me
£2,000 a grand lad looks after his Dad.

The mortgages were obtained by deception putting false wage slips and
p60s in, and the Building Societies as long as they got their big
Endowment Policy Payout they did not care. The idea was to let the
properties out to cover the mortgage and nobody would lose any money
as I had only borrowed 90% of their valuation. Most people put false
wages down otherwise nobody would get a mortgage.

Peter Mandelson M.P a government minister obtained a "Mortgage" For
£3000,000 he was not even charged I wonder if he was Freemason.
Helen did a £70,000 fraud herself it was a family concern every thing we
had went in to what I called the family pot every thing belonged to the
whole family, that's how I saw it. But weren't the bank's robbers
themselves go back to the Promenade Site when F.N.F.C. charged me
£10,000 penalties for 56 days or they would make me bankrupt and they
where charging me £15 per hour interest and that was 15 years ago,
back to the present day Natwest charging me 29% interest that is
daylight robbery, legal daylight robbery but robbery no less lets have it
right.   I sold houses to families on social security they claimed
housing benefit which covered more than the mortgage payments but
they would not pay the mortgage, they drank it instead.

One gentleman I took in to a mortgage broker, Roy Black he could not
remember how old he was, off his head on weed, he gave his occupation
as a bouncer at Mothercare he still got his mortgage. As long as the
building society got the endownment policy fee they turned a blind eye
Too cut a long story short I was arrested after being grassed on and
charged with obtaining 14 mortgages by deception £500,000 in total.
I was taken to Southport Police Station, I was questioned for hours by
Fraud Squad Officer Cuthbertson, I gave my name age and address and
said no comment to every other question, I was finger printed and
photographed, then released on bail.

I used Burton Copeland of Manchester for my defence not that I had
any, Mr Smyth was the solicitor who would look after me, he told me I
was looking at 4 to 6 years with a bit of luck depending on what Judge I
would get

Things were not looking to good a week later all the family were
arrested and taken to Formby Police Station, I said I had forged all their

signatures on the mortgage forms and they walked free with all charges dropped.

During the summer of 1993 I had to see Mr Smyth every week, he wanted a complete breakdown of what I had done since leaving school in 1955. It was my first offence in 56 years. I did the fraud to save my home and business if things had gone to plan all the 14 mortgages would have been paid, I only borrowed 90% of the value of the houses so I gave the Building Societies £600,000 worth of property on their own valuation and borrowed only £,500,000 they were quids in.

Unfortunately they did not look at it the same way as me.

"I will get you a good Q,C and Barrister unless you want to choose your own."

"How about George Carmen "I said hopefully.

"I don't think legal aid will run to that, I see you have still got your sense of humour, I have got Mr Stieger Q.C and Mr Campbell - George who will be your Barrister two good legal brains. Looking at the evidence everything is in black and white so you would be better pleading guilty, you will get a longer sentence if you plead not guilty and go for trial costing the taxpayer thousands of pounds."

" O.K I will plead guilty".

The police were trying to make it a big conspiracy trial they said there was 13 people involved,a total of £4,000,000 which would make things look worse, I only new 4 people out of the 13 I had never even met the other 9 .

About a month later we appeared at Southport Magistrates Court it was then passed on to the Liverpool Crown Court.

Mates you had known years as soon as they got in the police station grass on you to save their own skin they shit themselves, their nothing lower than a snake, yellow streak down their back.

Originally the police charged us with Conspiracy to Defraud Banks and Financial Institutions but this was a very old law and because we had not handled the money directly ourselves it was sent by wire or telex between banks and solicitors this law did not cover that modern aspect. I was on bail for 4 years altogether while they invented a new law. During this time I had to go to Crown Court in Liverpool Preston and Manchester 12 times we would wait all day not knowing if we were going to be imprisoned that day.

Helens obsession with the horses and animals had driven us apart she had at one time 15 pets I was the number 16. They had a survey in the Daily Mail on couples who had horses, they asked the wives if it come to the crunch who would they pick the horses or their husbands 70 out of a 100 picked the horse.

I was washing the car at the rear of the house, Helen was grooming one of her horses on the other side of the hedge She was brushing its mane "I do love you my darling my little love, oh my little love I do love you"

"I am over here Helen"

She snarled "I am talking to the horse"

Helen hardly left the place if we went out for a meal she would not go for a drink before or after she wanted to get back to the zoo. I asked her why she always turned her back on me in bed ".

She said " That's the way I want to sleep"

I would always turn to her put my arm around her she would not even hold my hand, knowing that you are wanted was more important than the sex .

On February 24th 1994 the Bank took us to the Southport County Court to repossess our Home and Cattery.

Helen left that morning with her friend Christine to go to see Patrick Swazees from Dirty Dancing he bred Arab Horses in South Carolina U.S.A. she came back after a couple of weeks then flew out to South Africa for month to see her parents.

I was in court trying saving the home, I told the judge I had a definite buyer for the property, I had sent a contract out to a friend of mine Ron Ellis and showed the Judge a letter from my solicitor confirming it.

Luckily he gave me 3 months to complete which saved the day.

The thousands of pounds spent on her holidays could have been paid into court. Helen thought we would lose the house so she would have a good time before eviction.

Helens bothers in law Pete and Harry were having a drink with me, we were playing pool in the lounge. Helen had gone out with her sisters Sheila and Cynthia.

Pete was in his cups after a good drinking session, he was getting upset, I asked him what was the matter.

"What can you do Eddie when you love someone and you can not get near them?"

I said "Join the club I am living like a Monk, how about you Harry when did you last get your leg over?"

Harry said "I can`t remember".

Must be a family trait. A week later just to put the top hat on it I got a letter of the taxman wanting £60,000.

My accountant Mr Norman Borton rang me and asked me if I would like to do some fire damage renovations on a property 50 The Promenade one of my old properties he was now the freeholder and responsible for the building insurance. He agreed a price of £27,739 the second floor front flat was completely gutted the stairs and landings were badly smoke damaged and the whole front off the flats needed painting. It took us 6 months to complete there were only my son Mark, Terry and myself we worked very hard and put many hours in working weekends as well. Borton was paying by stage payments the Insurance Company was satisfied with the work and paid Borton the full amount £27,739 He only paid me £15,786 and he still owes me that amount now plus all the interest and he new the state I was in.

I rang Mr Smyth of Burton Copeland who where acting for me in the fraud case. I explained how Borton had ripped me off. He said we would sue him " I have a young lady here who is brilliant at litigation her name is Miss MacAteer I will make a appointment for you at 2 p.m. tomorrow is that alright with you?"

"That is fine Mr Smyth". I caught the train at Southport I arrived at Burton Copelands office at Deansgate Manchester. I went to reception and asked for Miss McAteer she came out and introduced herself and escorted me to a small side office. She was Irish looked very young for a solicitor in her late twenties short and stocky with brown hair just above her shoulders. Her skirt was a bit short showing plenty of leg but I thought we have better legs on our table.

After explaining the situation she asked me why Horton had used a Limited Company instead of his own name. "I have no idea maybe he had something up his sleeve."

"Your other case is being paid for by Legal Aid but you will have to pay for this one yourself. I paid fees of £887 during the next 12 months. Miss McAteer who was only a Assistant Solicitor, some months later got Bortons Investments Ltd into Manchester County Court only to find that the company was put into receivership in 1992 some 3 years previously. A company search would have shown had she done one.

Miss McAteer now tells me she will sue him in his own name.

The case is now moved to Leigh County Court nearly a year later 6 –12-1996 Edward O`Brien v Neil Borton Horton does not turn up because his name is Norman. Unbelievable but true. This farce went on for another 3 years. During that 3 years Burton Copeland never got Borton in court.

I knew I was going to goal but not when, then all the banks would close in for the kill, we had a couple of options, we could sell the whole lot at

Formby the house cattery and the 8 acres and come away with cash or just sell the house for £170,000 which would clear our debts and keep the cattery and the £30,000 a year income. But Helen did not want to sell the cattery and stables must not upset the horses, so we split the deeds and put the house on the market for £155,000. But under the Married Women`s Act a bank can`t take the wife`s share of the house for her husbands business debts if it is in joint names.

I thought it would be a good idea to put the cattery in my youngest sons name Steven then it would be safe from Banks who I owed money to, we would take it back, when things got better, he was quite happy acting as trustee, a grand lad.

I put the Cattery in Stevens name because Eddie had a house and Mark had 3 houses, I had given Mark 50 Warwick Street the one I had in bought in 1974 for £200 it was now worth £38,000.

The Co-op bank wanted £75,000 to settle, Steven borrowed £55,000 off a bank on the Cattery and Mark lent us £20,000 he borrowed on 50 Warwick Street, so at least the Cattery was safe.

I hardly saw Helen always outside with the horses and the green wellie women all she worried about was losing the horses.

I met another women in 1994 called Christine and moved in with her I felt as though I was wanted not like the spare part some people thought she was rich but she worked a cake shop.

Some of the flats at Woodvale had been repossessed one I had sold for £45,000 was been sold for £18,000 why they drop in value so much after they have been repossessed ,

I can`t understand they are still the same flat. I knew a couple who had wanted a flat the year before but they could only raise £30,000

So I planned to buy it complete on the same day with them and the building society and make £12,000 profit. I arranged a viewing and offered the asking price of £18,000 which was accepted, I was buying it in a different name, I would buy and sell on the same day .

My sister Rosemary who lives in Formby said I looked tired and worried and she was worried about me She suggested I go to see Fr Short at Our Ladies Church at Formby and have a word with him. I was not a regular church goer, I had been in the past.

I called in to see Fr Short he invited me into the his house he was appalled that I had been on bail 4 years and my other problems, we knelt down and prayed together and he gave me a blessing .

You go now Eddie, don't worry about a thing the Lord is with you everything will go well from now on God is with you, have no fear you are in the hands of the lord.

On the following Monday I started to do some work on the flat .

The flat only needed decorating and painting outside I changed the locks and put a sold notice up to deter future punters. After the inside was finished I started to paint the outside I was about 12 feet up painting the woodwork when I over stretched and fell onto the concrete walkway landing on my left side. I tried to get up but could not, two young lads came up, Daren and Dale who lived nearby they rang for a ambulance it was the winter of 1995 November it was freezing cold lying on the concrete it was over 20 minutes before I heard the sirens of the ambulance coming in the distance, thank God for that I thought.

But when they got very near they stopped, it must have gone somewhere else. No it had a blow out around the corner the tyre had burst. That had to send for another this one came from Formby another 20 minutes I thought I was going to die of cold besides the other pain I was in. Leading up to the first floor walkway was a spiral stairway so they could not get a stretcher up so they had to put me in a chair it was agony I thought I would be dead before I got to the hospital.

At the rear of the ambulance I asked could they leave me in the chair, I found later that my femur had snapped in four places and the ball joint in my hip had broke in two, but they insisted I had to go on the bed it was horrific, when I was lying on the bed the driver started taking my blood pressure they were not Para Medics they had no pain killers or medicine with them.

"What are you doing, get me to the hospital" My leg is hanging off and he is taking my blood pressure .Arriving at Southport Hospital a nurse came and cut my overalls off and I was taken for x-ray then taken back to the reception area I was left on a trolley for what seemed like hours. Then a young Pakastani Doctor came over, He said " I have some good news and some bad news for you which do you want first?"

That's all you want is a comedienne "

I will give you the bad news first, you have shattered you hip and femur now the good news we can fix it"

I was taken down to the operating theatre and the put metal in my hip joint and a metal bar the length of my femur and screwed my bones to it. On Saturday at lunchtime, I had been in two days a young nurse come over. "Up you get, you will have to get up."

"Who me I can't get up I have only just come in."

"You have to get up"

"I am not getting up"

"The doctor will get you up"

The Doctor come down, I don't know were he is from but he is black as coal can hardly speak English "Up, up, up you must get up"

Anyway I got up and they sat me on a chair but my leg started to hurt with putting weight on it, I was soon in agony.

I thought sod this I am getting back into bed, I stood up and fell flat on my back, I had a blood clot a Pulmonary Embolism blocking my main artery, my head was fuzzy I seemed to be amongst clouds, I could not speak gasping for air The young nurse came over the doctor had gone she called the ward sister who came with a young male nurse with blue lapels on his jacket. I am lying on the floor, I can remember pulling at my pyjama collar trying to breath .

The male nurse said " He is going blue, he is going blue"

"You are right said the Ward Sister he is going blue"

I was fading, then coming back, the other patients were all looking down at me dying nobody doing anything, I thought if I am going blue it is my heart. I could hear them saying he has gone, another one said Eddie`s dead he is a goner get the priest quick he has stopped breathing.

I could hear them saying this but I could not answer.

I seemed to be floating in the clouds, was I dead, am I still alive I was looking around for Saint Peter it seemed an eternity, I thought it is not so bad being dead.

Then a German doctor who passing through the ward 9a he came over took one look and ran and got the oxygen bottle that was 10 feet away and put the mask over my mouth blew the clot from the lung entrance and saved my life.

Could not the Ward Sister have done this instead of watching me die you can excuse a young nurse freezing but not the Ward Sister.

Later that afternoon the German doctor came to see me.

"How are you, are a very lucky man I honestly thought that you were dead, another 10 seconds and I could have not saved you."

"I can`t thank you enough doctor you saved my life everybody else was watching me die, I will never forget you, many thanks "

Here is me calling the Germans for everything then one saves my life.

I was put on a machine which my blood passed through trying to catch this clot which was circulating my body it could block again anytime I was told never to cross my legs, what about when I was asleep I could cross them during the night then in the morning wake up dead.

The doctors gave me Warfarin which is rat poison, this thins the blood which hopefully will get past the clot, the doctors told me I had to drink

8 pints of water a day, the tablets I was taking were dehydrating me then I found I could not urinate after 3 days I told the male nurse, he got a plastic tube attached to a plastic bag And shoved this up the inside of my penis I nearly went through the roof. I had not been to the toilet for 12 days .

I could not use the bed pan, the doctor gave me some liquid and said " get to the toilet double quick"

I must have looked a site on my zimmer carrying a bottle of urine going as fast as I could the liquid did the trick, walking back from the toilet I noticed I was going over as I walked rocking from side to side, I stopped the nurse I explained that I was not walking straight.

I was limping

"That`s right, they had to cut two inches of your leg".

" I thought someone might have mentioned it"

I thought the doctors told you"

There was only eight patients in this ward 9a, end of November 1995 a new patient came in a man aged about 35 slight build he said he was having a operation to straighten his finger he said he would be out by lunch time.

The went down to the operating theatre about 9-30 a.m. came back about 11a.m. when he woke up he could not breath they had somehow punctured his lung. The nurse rang the panic bell and a surgeon came in and opened his chest to put a tube in but put it in the wrong side, he was screaming the place down, he was in for a month.

The following Saturday night about midnight there was a commotion in the ward the nurses were trying to get this big guy into bed he had just come in. He was over six feet big body builder skin head white tea shirt , build like Arnold Scharzenegger he was pushing the nurses around ,one of them gave him a needle, he was fast asleep.

Next morning stone dead he was on steroids and they had not checked, the hospitals bury their mistakes. I left the hospital and went back to Christines but left after a short time to go and live in one of my flats empty at Woodvale on my own.

A few doors away was a pub called the Sandpiper run by a couple of scousers called Bob&Sandra a nice friendly couple.   I was still on my crutches and I would hobble up to the Spar shop on Liverpool Road a couple of times Helen would be passing and she would stop and chat for a few minutes. A few months later after she stopped for a chat then asked me if I wanted to come back home, so I moved back to the family home Fernilea at Formby.

I still had to go to the Crown Court at Liverpool every couple of months while they were trying to sought this new Law out Helens younger sister Sylvia came back from South Africa after a mental breakdown, another Manic Depressant like her mother I asked her for the £1,000 I had lent her years before, she said I had not lent it to her but to her ex husband strange when I have never met him, never got it.

They say in the horsey world "Get a Horse and you get a Divorce."

In the evening what I call the "green wellie women" came around Margaret, Rebecca, Yvonne They would bring wine and drink what they had brought with them after they had finished that they would come over to the house were I would be watching television and ask me to go to the off license to get some more as they were over the limit to drive. Helens niece Hazel a collossus of a women, would join them.

She bought wine in a gallon sized plastic container we used to find her lying behind the settee or behind a fence she knew when she had enough, she just fell over, lovely girl.

When a foal was one year old they would bake a cake for it and put a banner across the stable "HAPPY BIRTHDAY BOBBY" they would go to the stable door and sing happy birthday to the foal who would run to the back of the stable terrified. They would go on holiday and send postcard back from Spain to the horses wish you were here, Mummy back soon what a sad lot.

It was the same in the cattery we would get Xmas cards, birthday cards and cards from Tennerife weathers nice, do miss you Felix see you soon. They would put the cat in the cattery after a tearful farewell some going back twice to say goodbye, they would get to Manchester Airport and ring up after only one hour " How is the cat?"

"It is dead" I would loved to have said that, just my sense of humour .

Finally I got my sentence date it was to be the 13 January 1997, they had come up with a new law or new charge which was Obtaining Valuable Commodities by Deception it had taken them 4 years to work this out, the original group of 13 were split into 5 and 8, I was in the five.

The solicitor who did over a £1,000,000 worth of conveyancing all on paper and the estate agent where not charged because they where Freemasons like most of the police and legal profession.

Some one must have done the paperwork verdict no case to answer.

It is not pleasant waiting on bail for 4 years looking at 4 to 6 years, there is a suicide every fourth day and a attempted suicide every other the United Kingdom prisons, but as they say you do the crime you do the time. I did not want anyone to go to court with me, you do not want you family watching you being sentenced Then taken down and handcuffed and chained to a prison officer.

On the court day Helen dropped me off at Woodvale post office I was getting a lift with my mate Sammy Gardner one of the accused his solicitors assistant Bob Cheatham was bringing him through from Southport. We had all pleaded guilty it was just a matter of being sentenced. Mr Stieger my Q.C told me the Judge Maddison was a very experienced Judge firm but fair.

There were 4 of us put in the dock, I was still on my walking stick.

"All Rise" shouted the court usher everybody stood up immediately. Judge Maddison sat up on his throne looking down on us it looked like a new wig he was wearing. He did a bit of a summary of the case he said "You have caused substantial financial losses to the Banks and Building societies and it was a serious crime that must be punished the maximum sentence for this offence is 10 years imprisonment".

That shook me as was expecting 4 to 6 years not 10, my mate Sammy Gardner was first to be sentence he got 2 years, next was Ted Cessford being the Grass he only got 180 hours community service.

I was next 21 months I was very relieved I was expecting 4 years at least. Dave Jones was next he got probation, the other lad got community service. Judge Maddison said the sentences would have been much harsher but for the time we had been on bail which was a sentence in its self this was caused by delays which were not of our making.

"Take them down"

When we got down below we were split up I was put in a cell with no windows I had just sat down when the light went out, a bit unnerving I just sat there after about 20 minutes the light came on, this was the screws sick joke. I was taken out and searched and they took my tie and belt off me.

We were then hancuffed to a warder taken out to a large prison van inside the van I was put in what I can only describe as a cupboard, more like a coffin you could hardly move there were no open windows the door was bolted top and bottom on the outside

If you were claustrophobic you would panic in fact they have opened these doors on a long trips and found prisoners dead. It was only a short trip to Walton Prison which was built over 200 years ago, I was glad to get out of the cupboard I was handcuffed again and led into the reception.

I had a shower and then the doctor and then to the cell, on the way I had to pick some blankets up, as I picked a roll up another prisoner said

" Take two rolls granddad you will be cold" with my walking stick and grey hair I must have looked the part.

There are 4floors on top of each other on each wing looking down onto a basement courtyard which is covered by wire mesh ceiling.

As I crossed the courtyard I could hear fighting and screaming I looked up through the wire mesh there were 4 men beating this other men his face was covered in blood they were kicking him, his face was getting beaten to a pulp ,he was screaming " No more no more"

I thought they were going to kick his head off ,it was getting booted from side to side, one eye socket was out on his cheek I stood there looking up motionless, they picked him up and threw him over the rail from the fifth floor he came hurtling down to land on the wire mesh just above my head, spots of blood landed on my blankets.

The wire mesh saved his life, apparently he had taken some ones burn (tobbaco). The screw said move on giving me a prod in the back, we went down a flight of stairs into a wide corridor there was no natural light, it was dark a very small bulb every 20 feet these were not cells they are dungeons.

" Stand there" he snarled, he opened the heavy metal door.

" Get in"

This was K Wing on the Ones .The cell was 5 feet wide, 12 feet long the ceiling about 14 feet high there was a barred window about 12 feet high. There were two metal bunks, next to the bunk was a toilet and a wash basin, that was it. The door was slammed behind me, I felt it vibrate through my body, there was a young lad of about 18 lying on the lower bunk. "Alright, I am John from Garston, you are on the top"

"Eddie I live in Formby" we shook hands. I made my bed then lay on the top, the mattress stank of urine the cell smelled damp and musty.

I am glad I got those extra blankets the only heat was a 4 inch pipe running through the cell .I just lay there thinking I would have to spend another 330 days and nights in here.

John my cellmate was doing 28 days for contempt of court he was finding it hard going. There was nothing in the cell no books or newspapers, nothing, after lying there for about 4 hours I said to John what time do you get to go out.

He just laughed "You don't get out, it is 23:1/2 lock up in here, you can go out on to the exercise yard for 30 minutes but if you go out on your own you will get your head kicked in you only have to look at some one or say the wrong thing and you get a good kicking.

The door was opened at 5:30 for our tea I was given a metal tray split into three sections and I joined a long queue. I don't think we will get a menu, it was curried peas and rice yes that is right peas curried sauce and rice all mixed together.

With an apple and a cup of stewed tea, with a blue tinge you could not drink it. Then straight back to be locked up again The prisoners made lines they ripped sheets up into strips then they tied a plastic mug on the end, they put drugs in or burn and pass messages these lines would be swung from the window, cell to cell and would travel the length of the wing on the back wall.

Time was dragging we just lay there you could hear the prisoners shouting to each other out of there cell windows most of the prisoner were between 18 and 35 some were regulars and new each other well so formed there own gangs for protection and beatings.

At 56 I felt vulnerable and threatened it was certainly a young mans game. My young cellmate John tried to cheer me up, he told me about his mate who was sentenced on the same day for burglary, his mate was expecting 12 to 18 months, but the judge had other ideas.

"I sentence you to 4 years imprisonment .His mate was shocked "
I can`t do 4 years your honour"

The judge leaned foreword and said " Well, just do what you can"

He told me the tale about the prisoner getting hanged in here in the 1950s, it was a cold January morning 8 am the prisoner was taken from his cell, he had to walk right across the exercise yard to the scaffold were Peirepoint the Hangman was waiting it was freezing cold, snow sleet and ice.

He turned to the warder alongside of him and said " What a morning to die it is cold wet and freezing"

"You are all right said the warder I have to walk back in this"

Next morning up at 7 a m out on the landing to queue for our breakfast a slow long line, there must be over 2000 men in here.

The largest prison in Europe and one of the toughest. It was corn flakes and 2 rounds of toast the tea was like piss, time dragged on John had been locked up 24 hours a day for 3 weeks he was only 18 years old.

It is embarrassing going on the toilet in front of some one but you had to do, same when they went on. John left the following week I got a new cell mate a drug addict you can always tell a drug addict their face is white as a sheet and usually very thin. He was called Barry from Manchester he looked dreadful his hands were shaking he was nodding his head. "I need fix man I need a fix" In prison when they are coming down off drugs they call them Rattlers, at night they shake so much that they grip the sides of the metal bunk bed and rattle all night until some one smacks them in the mouth. Barry had brought a Daily Mirror in it was a few days old but it was great having something to read.

You are allowed a 1hour visit each week, Helen and Mark were coming in to see me on Wednesday afternoon, and I was really looking forward to it. I was escorted to the visiting room and sat at a table waiting for Helen and Mark, there were raised voices at the next table next thing the prisoner punched the women opposite him, her nose burst open blood all down her white nylon blouse.

Then the man she was with butted the prisoner he went down then other prisoners joined in blood everywhere.

Every body seemed ready to explode at the least thing.

Next thing, the Mufty Squad come in to sort them out ,the a warders some of the 6ft 6in to 6ft 8in 18 to 20 stone they sorted all out in a couple of minutes, they are called the Mufty Squad because during the day some of the prisoners on drugs give the warders verbal abuse, and they know the warders cannot kick them in front of witnesses.

So the Mufty Sqad come around after lights out and give them a severe kicking the warders muffle their boots, hence the name.

Helen and Mark came in there was still blood on the chair by the next table. "What`s that's Eddie?" Helen asked pointing to the blood.

"There was a bit of a scuffle Helen" I think she was shocked by the conditions she came out with a classic.

"You will have to get out of here"

"I will go and see the Governor when I go back."

There was a prisoner sitting there on his own, he had been what is known as Ghosted his visitors had not turned up, he had to sit there for a hour every body looking at him. You can`t walk out it is a terrible thing to do too a prisoner.

Back in the dungeon my cellmate Barry had also been on a visit he looked a little happier actually smiling. "Where is that newspaper Eddie?"

I passed him the Daily Mirror, he spread it on the floor, dropped his trouser and shit on it.

" Sorry about this " he said as he squatted there grimacing, ah it is coming "

A load of diarrhoea spread across the paper he put his fingers in the diarrhoea and routed around. "I don't think it has come out yet" He squatted down again over the paper, his face was contorted a he struggled to shit "Oh oh" he moaned Another load of diarrhoea splashed down on to the paper, he put his fingers in and had another route around, "Ah here it is, "he held up a shit covered condom which had his drugs in it. When they kiss their wives or girl friends in reception they pass on the condom, which they swallow.

The prison is awash with drugs how do they get in do the solicitors bring them in the warders or the visitors, is a blind eye turned because it keeps the prisoners quiet.

I asked the Screw who unlocked us for dinner, could I change my mattress as it was smelly and covered in piss stains.

" No fucking chance, do you think this is Butlins"

Barry had fell asleep on the floor after one of his fix`s, so I swapped mattresses with him, he would not notice, he could not remember coming in.

Another week and Barry was moved out, in moved a lad from Newcastle he was a massive skin head covered in tattoos he had magpies and Newcastle United tattooed on his arms and a Eagle covered his chest. He looked a mean bastard, you don`t know who will share your cell next

"What are you in for?"

" Mortgage fraud"

"How much?"

"Half a million"

" Must have been a big house"

"There was more than one, sorry what`s your name?"

"Mark, they call me Mark the Nark"

"What are you in for?"

"Manslaughter my brother and I kicked this lad to death they tried to pin a murder charge on us, I got 8 years, my second manslaughter charge I have already done a 5 year stretch."

He seemed proud of his deeds the one who does most crime or the worst crime is classed as top dog.

I was told by one of the more friendly screws that I might be moved to a more open prison at Kirkmam near Blackpool it was for non-violent prisoners. He said it was a working prison and you had to be fit no medical problems. Unfortunately the blood clot in hospital was classed as a heart attack and my gammy leg would not help.

I think the idea is that the first couple of weeks in prison are made as hard for you as possible to see if you will crack up, you see grown men crying asking for their mothers and all they get is abuse or a hiding of other prisoners, you have to be mentally strong more than physically strong, some just cant hack it as big and hard as think they are.

Some prisoners are very helpful they show you how to commit suicide, don't slash your wrists across the vein slash them length ways then they cant save you. I have known people go into hospital on the outside that found the going to tough for them and signed themselves out.

Mark the Nark was moved out and a lad called Terry moved in He was from Eccles near Manchester, he was in for car crime and theft. He had a pack of cards so that passed a bit of time.

Things were getting a little better we could watch television for 1 hour at night some screws would leave the doors open for half an hour and you could talk to other prisoners. When you see prisons on T.V. you see them all playing pool or in the gym all day all having a great time they want to come in here to Walton. I went to see my landing officer to see if I could go to Kirkham the open prison, he said I could not go if I had medical problems, but I could appeal to the Governor myself, I put a appeal in and got a appointment with the Governor two days later.

The Screw escorting me to the Governors said" You are to old to be in here mate, they will kill you they are fucking animals".

Inside the Governors office there were a panel of 6 men I explained that when I came in I played on my ailments hoping to go to the Hospital Wing, but I was quite fit and used to building work it was not a heart attack I had in hospital but a Pulmonary Embolism.

I had left my walking stick in my cell

They could not decide, but said if I see another doctor and he passed me I could go. I had to wait another couple of days, and it was a English doctor he examined me looked at my medical card and said

"I am afraid I can not let you go to a working prison what if you dropped dead we would all be in trouble, you have had a heart attack "

"Yes but that was caused by the operation if I had not had that operation, I would not had the blood clot. He was on the point of turning me down, when a women screw that was working in the office said

"Oh, let the old bugger go, you would not like to be in this hell hole at his age, if he dies he dies they will probably kill him here anyway."

He passed me, another 3 days and I was on my way, back in the dreadful sweat box in seemed strange going through your own town in a prison van, people doing there shopping families out together things you don't cherish until you lose them. It took a couple of hours to get there, Kirkham was a R.A.F camp during the war it covered many acres

There were different factories with private management a turnover of millions of pounds, it had a farm were they grew the vegetables for other prisons, there was a Timber Department were fitted kitchens were

made, garden sheds furniture. Denim jeans and shirts were produced.
I was glad to get out of the sweatbox .

I was handcuffed to a screw and taken into the reception area there
were 12 of us altogether. There were about 12 wooden huts divided into
16 cells the walls only went up about 10 feet then there was a gap
between the ceiling the cells were bigger than at Walton 2 single beds
either side of the cell.

A toilet block at the far end. I was allocated a cell in hut 3 there was
nobody about only the cleaner who is locked in all day while the others
are at work. It was like winning the pools to get out of Walton .

I had not seen a bird or a tree for months the little things in life you take
for granted. It was good to be able to look out of the window, there
were dozens of ducks wandering about when it was mealtime the ducks
would follow the prisoners to the canteen. They would wait and the
prisoner would give them bread when they came out, they had a rule if
you hit a fellow prisoner you got 28 days, if you kicked a duck you got 56
days.   The prisoners worked from 8 a.m. until 5 p.m. tea at 5.30
p.m. then you were free until lock up at 9.30 p.m. You could play football
go to the gym but there was 800 men trying to get on the equipment,
there was a library. You were allowed to mix outside but you could not
visit another block and go inside I suppose this was to prevent drug
dealing.   This prison in the past was known as a soft prison.
Prisoners could nip over the fence and go to the chippie

There was plenty of drink passed over the fence at night. But now they
have C.C.T.V these cameras can tell what size vest you are wearing day
or night.

One prisoner got his wife to tie drugs around his dogs neck and put him
under the fence, he whistled the dog got the drugs of it but the dog
would not leave him and go back and he got caught.

The first night was bedlam, had I jumped out of the frying pan into the
fire most of the prisoners were teenagers their heads shaven to make
them look hard.

A lot of them on drugs, how they got them God only knows, after lock up
they all put the radios on music blasting out from each cell all on
different stations all trying to drown each others music.

Then to top it all the Pakistani's would join in. Then they would find
someone who had shit or pissed in there bed to settle a score, they
would go to who they thought had done it then the fights would start,
they would be radios and chairs flying through the air, screams of lads
getting beaten up, young lads getting raped.

Hell on earth.

Things quiet end down about 1 A.M but there were still a couple of radios on, I could not get asleep. It was the same every evening they called this part of the prison the Bronx no wonder.

They had other hobbies like making paper planes out off newspapers they would light the tail and throw them over the partition. They would glide over a couple of cells then land on somebody who was asleep this was great fun for the lads. The other practical joke was to set lads on fire this was hilarious, all the prisoners wore thin nylon boilers suits for work, if you were waiting in a queue they would set your arse on fire with their lighters they would run after you and put you out, what great fun.

Only 262 days to go I felt as though I had been in here for years, when you see in the paper some one get 6 or 12 months it does not seem a long sentence but try doing it.

You could ring home once a week I wrung Helen one afternoon she said "Jack`s here "

"Jack who"

" The builders rep"

 Must have come around for a brew

I had been given a office job because of my medical condition booking fruit and vegetables in we were paid £7 per week but you had to spend it in the shop on phone card shaving soap tea bags etc, I could not eat the breakfast because everything was cooked the night before even the toast, so I bought loads of corn flakes had them for my breakfast and tea and went to the canteen for my lunch.

There would be a couple of hundred in the queue if it was raining you would get soaked before you got served the portions could have not been smaller. The food was pigswill. One day a new lad came in still in his teens he sat on our table, he had finished his dinner in no time,
" You don`t get much to eat do you"

One of the old lags said "If you are still hungry son go up and ask for seconds, see that screw behind the counter".

The young lad got up and went over to the counter they had just finished serving. "Excuse me sir could I have some seconds?"

The canteen fell silent, "You taking the piss?" he grabbed the young lad by the lapels of his donkey jacket Lifted him halfway across the counter, "Now you fuck off before I put you in the block".

I caught the Flu very badly my lips were purple and I was shivering and shaking I felt really ill I asked my boss if I could go back to my cell to lie down. The block was locked up, I went in to the screws office to ask him

if I could get in to lie down, they just laughed get back to fucking work
the doctor only comes once a week and he was here yesterday.
I had to go back to work so I stayed in the cloakroom.
I felt really ill I could not eat. With the noise of the radios the fighting
and screaming I was ready to die, I coughed all night hardly slept. I went
to the so called clinic in the morning run by a screw with a white doctors
coat on. He was the image of Basil Faulty no matter what was wrong
with you, you got 2 aspirins there was of course a long queue, the man
in front of me was next he explained to the screw who was called Doctor
Death that he was cracking up he said he could not handle prison life he
said he could not sleep and started to cry I will kill myself"
Doctor Death said "If you can`t sleep son, lie on the edge of the bed you
will soon drop off",
He gave him 2 aspirins "Now piss off".
I got 2 aspirins as well. I had to go to work, shivering and sneezing,
I got through the day and in the evening a West Indian gave me a small
onion, his said cut it up and put it in a cup of boiling water, let it soak
then drink it. I stayed in bed, about 8 p.m. 3 skinheads came in."
If you start coughing tonight mate and keep us awake like last night we
will come and kick your teeth in, be warned.
" The next morning I felt great the onion had worked a treat
That night at about 11 p.m. there was a scouser shouting and arguing, he
had been out on day release which you get at the end of your sentence
he had come back blind drunk and had smuggled half a bottle of whisky
in. He was staggering down the corridor, with cells either side shouting
" Where are the Packies dirty bastards Come out you dirty bastards, shit
all over the toilets, shit all over the pan won`t sit down after a white
man. Some of the prisoners we shouting
"There`s no black in the Union Jack In their Koran they class us as
Infidels, and stand up to shit, "Come out you black bastards".
My cell mate was a Packistani, Rasheed from Manchester he looked
terrified, quick Rasheed get under my bed, he had just got under when
my cell door was kicked open.
" where are the packi bastards?
Some one shouted from the far end of the block." Come down here you
white twat and I will fuck you"
The Scouser staggered down to the other shouting," Black bastards,
black bastards"
When he got down the far end someone shouted from the other end "
Come down here you white trash white shithouse"

He was up and down the corridor like a lunatic.

It was 2 other scousers winding their mate up shouting abuse, this defused the situation, but the next evening there was a 100 Pakistanis at the block wanting to sort the Scouser out but lucky for him the screws had moved him out.

It is true Pakistan`s won`t sit down after a white man, the toilet doors are only half the size of normal doors, so if there is a queue people are watching you on the toilet and you can see the pakistan`s standing or crouching and they shit all over the pan.

This filthy habit creates bad feeling amongst the other prisoners.

The violence was everywhere there were fights in the dinner queue, on the football field in the gym.

There was 2 older men then me, one was in a wheel chair the other one was in the next block. Some one said this old chap was a Nonce a child molester, 4 young prisoners took him around the back of the block and gave him a severe beating they broke his ribs put the boot in and his cheek bone smashed, he was put in Intensive Care at Blackpool Infirmary. He had not paid his council tax and not abused children

The 4 thugs were sent to a closed prison at Preston the screws locked all the prisoners the in their block in for 24 hours until they were forced out by other prisoners

After 3 months I was moved off the Bronx to a better part of the prison, these were brick built cells but you had your own cell and the walls went up to the ceiling you had your own key to your cell but of course .the main door was locked, there was a better television room and shower room. I also had a change of job I was moved to the Warp Prep this was were they did the yarn for the denim jeans but It was very boring all the part rolls of yarn that were left. We had to make one big one by tying the ends together with a little gadget then put on a machine to make one big roll, the money was the same. You could enroll on a cookery course or a computer course anything to pass the time.

Helen would visit me every week my sons Eddie, Mark and Steven 3 grand lads and my mate Bernard. This would give you something to look foreword to I had my diary and every morning I would cross another day off I had done 300 days now it seemed like 300 years 20 days to go, thank God.

At last the day of my release 27 November 1997, Helen met me at the gates, it was like winning the Pools, we drove through Preston,.

I thought when we get home Helen would cook me to a nice big home cooked breakfast I was really looking forward to it, but she took me to a cafe instead. Could not be bothered to cook for me.

When I got home my 3 dogs came racing out to greet me, even Oliver the goat was calling I went over to see him he put his feet up on my chest and made a great fuss. My 3 sons were there, it was great to be home you don't know what you have until you miss it.

Helen had her own little zoo 6 horses 7 cats 3 dogs and a goat. We got on great together, never closer, it was like a new Beginning, I was so glad to be home I hardly went out.

Still under pressure from the banks I had put the Cattery in Stevens name in 1995 until things got better, now the Natwest were coming after the house so I asked Steven if we could put the house in his name as well. This is so the Banks can't get them they had been trying to repossess the house since 1992 they told us to put it on the market but because of the structural faults it was unmortgageable and we never had one offer.   Helen said she had been offered £170.000 for the house from her friends Margaret and Rebbecca this was fantastic news we could pay off the Bank and stay put.

The Bank said they would send their own surveyor down, he came looked at the house which had dropped at least 9 inches at one end, and valued it at £55,000 but he had missed the planning permission I had obtained in the field adjoining the house, it was worth more than the house, it had planning for a Boarding Kennels for 72 it was like gold 72 dogs at £10 per day £720 per day £5,040 per week £150,000 for 30 weeks out of the year it was worth a £100,000.

I said to Steven, grand lad that he is "The bank are going to take the house Steven can we put it in your name like we did the Cattery in 1995?",.

"Yes, but I want £20,000 plus a plot of land to build a house on".

"How do you mean?".

"If I don't get the £20,000 plus the plot of land I won't do it."

I could not believe what I was hearing my own flesh and blood blackmailing me, my son who I had worked hard for to send to private school.

" Let me get this right Steven, you are blackmailing us your own father and mother for £20,000 and if we don't pay you will see us evicted and out on the street ".

"That's right no money no deal."

" You fucking shit house, you fucking scum bag, you are fucking shite, get out I would rather lose the house than be blackmailed by my own son. Helen said" Don't worry I would sort him out".

I did not realize at the time they were working together behind my back. Helen and I had an agreement that if we split up I would have the house and piece of land for the dog kennels, she would have the cattery the stables and 6 acres of land plus the £35,000 income of the cats. I was getting a third and she was getting 2 thirds but I did not mind her getting more.

Helen then informs me that her 2 friends had withdrawn their offer and did not want to proceed with the purchase of our home.

I knew that when we got to court we would be evicted from the house we had scraped through so many times before and the courts were sick of me turning up. Steven had me up against the wall if I did not succumb to his blackmail, we would lose the house and time was running out.

The Bank said they would settle for £75,000 but the Yorkshire Bank put a caution on it for money I owed from the flats so they said they would settle for £2,000 a total of £77,000. About £100,000 would have cleared all our debts. The £60,000 was still owed to the tax man fact if we could get my accounts done we would not owe any tax.

Helen said she had got Steven down to £10,000, I felt like shooting the bastard it was either that or losing our home. So we signed contracts this got the bank to stop proceeding they did not know who was buying it. Now that every thing was in Stevens name Helen went on the turn.

A girl who Helen called Liz came around every evening about 5:30p.m. she had Poodle Parlour shop in Formby but it had closed down, she was looking for new premises for dog grooming. I was cooking the tea every night, I was just about to put the 2 plates on the dining table at the rear of the house in walks Liz no knock, I had the plates in my hand.

"We are just about to have our tea Lo".   "

That's alright". And walked pass me and went in to see Helen They came out a little later,

" Your teas on the table love"

" Put it in the oven, I will have it later" They went out into the Cattery, Liz had brought some wine, then big Hazel the South African niece would come around, built like a man and could drink enough for two, then Margaret and her friend Rebecca would turn up with their bottles they would be on the booze all evening. I cooked the tea the next night, Helens outside with Lo I went out and shouted .

"Your teas ready Helen "

"Put it in the oven" This happened the next few nights, I told her the next morning that it is no good doing you tea if you did not eat it.

"Well just do your own then"

" I never see you now, you are always out in the stables or Cattery"
"The horses are my life, if you don't like you can lump it".
In all the 33 years we were married she had never come to me she was
as cold as ice. As soon as that Liz showed her face everything between
Helen and I went downhill Helen came in just after midnight pissed as
usual. " Who`s this fucking slag ringing you every fucking night?"
I was a bit taken aback" I don't know what you mean".
"I will show you what I mean its on the Cattery answer phone, come out
here and I will play it back to you"
The Cattery extension line was in the kitchen, she turned it on. A
women`s voice said "Hello Helen is Eddie there if he is not I will ring
again."
" Who is that"?
" I have no idea who it is".
"She knows your fucking name so she must know you, she has rung 3
nights this week.
"Honestly, I have no idea who she is".
This confrontation carried on every night; I did not have a clue who that
women was.
"She has rung again you scum bag, get out of here and get yourself a
flat, you must know who it is" .
At about 11p.m. Friday night Cattery extension phone rang in the
kitchen I answered it was a females voice saying.
" Have you just rang this number?"
I said" No the Cattery is closed at the moment if you leave your number I
will get Helen to ring you back in the morning."
She gave me the number a Skelmersdale number I wrote it down on the
pad and went to bed to miss the lunatics piss head.
Next morning I told Helen about the number on the pad, the women
who had been making the phone calls was from Skelmersdale.
Helen had dialed 1471 it was a Skelmersdale number. I could not think of
anyone I new there, then it came to me the only person it could be was
Vera the couple I had sold the house to over the road, she had moved in
with her boyfriend Roy and 2 daughters and a son. Roy was goaled for
child sex abuse, the little girl ended up epileptic he was leaving the
mothers bed with her knowledge and going into her daughter`s bed
most nights of the week. We reported him to the Police he got 6 months
did 3 months for ruining the little girl life .the mother stood by the
abuser, the little girl came to live with us.
A couple of years later he died of cancer, the house was repossessed she

moved to Skelmersdale, but this was about 5 years ago, why start to cause trouble now. I went for a pint in the Sandpiper at Woodvale I met a mate of mine called Graham I told him about the phone calls and I thought it was Vera he said he thought he had her number in a old diary. I asked him would he ring me up when he got home, he did it was the same number.

Helen came in," Has that fucking slag rang you yet scum bag"

"No but I know who that fucking slag is, it is the dog who lived over the road Vera who was living with the pervert Roy I got her number of Graham it is the same number as what is on the pad, alright piss head, it is nothing to do with me, I have not seen her since she left over 5 year ago."

Helen went out and rang the number, giving her plenty of abuse, she never rang again. But no apology. Helen now tells me she has a buyer for the house her 2 girl friends who stable their horses here Margaret and Rebecca, have decided to buy our house after all. I have been stitched up good style by Helen and Steven working together, she already had these buyers waiting and delayed the sale until the house was in Stevens name and I would have no say in it this is why she wants me out of the house. Helen started the nightly tirade of abuse coming in pissed up.

" Who is this other slag ringing, more fucking calls come out here and I will play it back to you fucking scum bag"

She put the cattery answer phone on, a females voice was screaming and shouting. "The Gypsies were going to get you Helen, going to kill you. "Now then whose that fucking slag?"

"I have no idea who it is like I had no idea who the last one was".

It turned out to be her niece Hazel ringing up for a laugh.

"The sooner your out of here the better get yourself a flat"

"I am going nowhere" Helen went to the Lakes for 10 days with her sister Cynthia, a couple of days after she came back. I was sitting in the front lounge watching the television, and she kicks off again.

"Who`s this women you have been seen with in our car?"

" I have had no women in the car, I have not been out only to the Spar shop I have seen no one"

"My friend saw you with a women in the car ".

"When was this?"

"Before I went away"

" You are telling me you have waited nearly two weeks before you mentioned it. Nobody would wait 2 weeks if they caught their husband in a car with another women especially you".

You tell your friend to come and face me tell me when, what day, what time, what place, face to face."

"Oh, no I am not getting her involved."

"You can`t just accuse me and not bring this friend of yours to face me"
A few days later she comes in screaming" I have cigarette stumps in the car with lipstick on them."

" Where are they then?"

" I have thrown them away, anyway I want you out of here go and get a fucking flat, it is not your house now it is Stevens house now you have no right to be in here I will get the police to throw you out."

I have had enough, so I moved into a small flat in Part Street in the town centre I was there a few months and started a computer course I had leant a little about computers when I was in prison, it was 9 a.m. until noon. I had done 3 weeks, I came home to find my front door had been kicked in my drawers and cupboards ransacked my Building Society Book and Passport stolen, that all I could see was missing.

I pulled the door too and dashed down to the Building Society to tell them, I only had £100 in the book.

When I got back to the flat my television and video recorder had gone robbed twice in one day.

The house was full of drug addicts and dealers, I asked the Landlord Mike Bold if he had any better houses out of the town centre.

He moved me to a nice quiet flat at 36 Lathom Road down by the Golf Course. A few months after Helen and Steven sold our house for £158,000 to Helen`s girlfriends Margaret and Rebecca, she had these buyers up her sleeve. Helen had waited until it was in Stevens name How did Steven get the loan of £57,000 off the bank he had no salary for a loan that size the cattery was not taking enough income wise .

I said to Helen the only way to get the loan was to find an accountant to do a set of false accounts to justify the loan without them we would be homeless. I found one for her He wanted £2,000 .

Helen agreed she sent off the cattery accounts they sorted them out Steven took them to the bank and they lent him £57,000

Helen refused to pay for them the cattery accounts were in her name. I was getting threats off the accountant without the accounts I had arranged she would not have got the loan.

The £60,000 we owed the tax the accounts were in joint E& H O`Brien the   tax man threatened me with bankruptcy .I wrote to them explaining that I had been forced out of my home had had a accident had Deep Veign Thrombosis also a Pulmonary Emberlism and my only income was £51 per week   on benefits . I sent them my medical reports and that I would not be able to work again at my age.

Seeing the accounts were in joint names .   .

They demanded the £60,000 off Helen her solicitor wrote to me for help I wrote back and explained that the only properties in Helens name were the ones she lived in which tax was exempt the properties being our home ,all the other properties I bought and sold were in my name only. They withdrew the demand . Not even a thank you

Remember the section of the Cattery Helen insisted leaving empty, she has had that converted into a bungalow for herself, remember her opening the Cattery bank account in her name only now we know why. Nothing was paid off the joint account it all went into her account.

Love is blind I was stupid never trust anyone and I mean anyone.

Helen and Steven now had the Cattery worth £300,000 plus the income, £35,000

I am on income support £51 per week.

 I said to Helen the only way to get the loan was to get an acountant to do a false set of accounts that would justify the loan without them we would be homeless   but she would not pay for them

She gave Steven £10,000 he put it down on his house at Alma Road Birkdale.

I divorced her on the grounds of unreasonable behavior, another Manic Depressant.

You would have thought if it was true that her friend who said had caught me in a car with a women, Helen would have divorced me for adultery. Her imaginary friend would have to give evidence on oath.

I asked my other 2 sons Eddie and Mark if they would come to court and tell the truth and not take sides but they would not believing their manic mothers lies, they sat on the fence.

I they had come to court I would have got half of the property I had in fact worked 45 years for nothing

In all the years we were married Helen never worked until she got the cattery, then she had a women to run it. I always thought I had been a good father and good provider and had taken a lot on over the years, put my head on the line for my family.

I could not work this situation out. My Solicitor Janice Lawler said our assets would be sorted out under the Ancillary Rights Act.

The Judge at Southport Court asked me. "What assets have you got Mr. O`Brien ?"

"I have nothing I am on Income Support. £56 per week

"And you Mrs O`Brien" "

I have none, I only earn £80 in the Cattery I work for my son."

In fact she earns £800 per week.

"Well if you both have nothing how can I split nothing"

"I put the property in my sons name as trustee"

"Were is the contract with your son"

"I did not think I would need one with my son, you don't expect your wife and son to rip you off after you have been married for 33 years."

"Evidently you do, I am afraid this case will have to go the Chancery Court in London it takes years to be heard ".

This is what I am waiting for now. In the meantime I sit here abandoned alone and broke. With both of us claiming Legal Aid we would not get a court hearing because they only give legal aid to one side of the dispute. We never did get to court. Happy Days.

It is not much fun living on £56 per week counting you money before you get to the supermarket till.

I had to sign on at the Job Centre but no one will give you a job at my age 58 and being an ex-convict. I was stuck in a rut.

After a while Helens solicitor sent me a cheque for £ 20,000 I had to give the acountant £2000 for cooking the books the rest I owed on the joint account'

I had started my Autobiography in long hand and filled many writing pads then I bought a second hand computer for £40. I could only type with one finger it took ages to do a single page. I would do a bit then go back and do a bit more it took me a couple of years to get the first draft together.

I asked my friend Ron Ellis who is a published Author if he could help me. He said it was rubbish and could not assist me.

Being desperate for cash I Thought I would ring Miss McAteer the Litigation Expert to see if she had sorted Borton out yet.

Or at least got his name right. I was informed Miss McAteer was no longer with Burton Copeland. Talking to a friend of mine, you don't have many left when you are broke he suggested I would be better off suing the solicitors Burton Copeland than Borton.

Not being an Asylum Seeker I could not get Legal Aid so I went to Southport County Court and issued A Summons it cost about £300. I had to cash in my last Insurance Policy to raise the cash.

After Burton Copeland received the Summons they offered me £10,000 to settle out of court I refused it was now 7 years since they took my case they now owed me £19,000 with charges and interest. They clearly did not want to go to court if they had paid me in 1995 the £12,000 I could have used that money to make money.

The court date was set for 4 day Of December 2002. Claimant Edward O`Brien and Defendants Burton Copeland.

Before Judge Field Q.C sitting at the Law Courts Albert Road Southport. Claim no DC200116 IT was a nice sunny morning cold but dry I arrived at the court at 9.30.A.M give me time to look at my papers. It was a change to be the Claimant in a court case as I was always the defendant. I was quite confident they had not even got Borton to court in nearly 4 years if this was not negligence nothing was.

In the waiting room their Barrister came over he was wearing his Wig and Gown he was trying to intimidate"

Now Mr O'Brien have you anything you want to say?"

"No I will have my say in court"

Little did he know I had probably been in court as many times as him. We were called into court their was the Usher and a couple of clerks. I was in the left hand front bench their Barrister was in the right front bench. "All Stand" bellowed the Usher. Mr Field Q.C. sat high up on the Judges Bench."

"Be seated"

"Now Mr O`Brien you take the stand and just say in your own words what has transpired take your time I know it is difficult representing yourself". I thought what a nice friendly Judge.

I gave evidence until 12 noon when had to break for dinner.

Mr Field Q.C. was very patient and helped me when I got tongue tied. I felt more confident now. We resumed at 2 p.m. It was their Barrister's turn to Question me.

"Good afternoon Mr O`Brien how are you?"

"I am fine thank you"

Another nice man I was thinking but not for long.

"Don`t forget Mr O`Brien you are on Oath, now then we had trouble finding your address Mr O`Brien didn`t we but we did find you after you had been in Prison is that correct Mr O`Brien."

I turned to face the Judge. "That is correct Your Honour but I thought this was a civil matter my past has nothing to do with this civil case today." My friendly Judges face had turned to thunder, if looks could kill. "Get on with it only speak to answer questions " He snarled.

I was not feeling to confident now. It was now 3-30 p.m. I was giving as good as I got because I was telling the truth he was fabricating.

Miss McAteer was brought into the witness box to be questioned by thier Barrister. She looked quite shifty looking down at the floor, she would not look at me. "Is it true Miss McAteer that you had great difficulty getting money and information off Mr O`Brien and he never answered your letters and telephone calls in fact very uncooperative and that most of the delays were down to him?"

"That is true Sir "

They continued to criticize me for another 10 minutes.

Then it was my turn to question Miss McAteer.

"Miss McAteer I believe you are not employed by Burton Copeland now". "That is correct"

"In fact Miss McAteer you are no longer in the Legal Profession at all is that correct?"

"Yes" "You were in control of this case for 4 years during those 4 years did you ever get the defendant Mr Horton anywhere near a Court?" "No"

"So Miss McAteer during those 4 long years you were a complete waste of time is that true. "Yes"

At least she was honest. "All stand" The Judge went to a room at the rear of the court to decide on the verdict. He returned about 20 minutes later. "All stand"

"It is ordered that Judgement be in favour of the Claimant Mr Edward O`Brien."

I have won I have one I will get £19,000 this was going through my head I was delighted I mean ecstatic.

" I will now decide on costs. There will be judgement on the claim for the Claimant in the sum £5. The Claimant to pay to the defendants £1,495

IN THE SOUTHPORT COUNTY COURT   Claim No.DC200116

BETWEEN :-

EDWARD O'BRIEN   <u>Claimant</u>

and

BURTON COPELAND   <u>Defendants</u>

Before Mr Recorder Field QC sitting at the Law Courts, Albert Road, Southport on 4th December 2002.

UPON hearing from the Claimant appearing in person and Counsel for the Defendants AND UPON hearing the evidence

IT IS ORDERED THAT:-

1.   There be judgement on the claim for the Claimant in the sum of £5.

2.   The Claimant do pay to the Defendants' the sum of £1,495 which sum is comprised as follows:

    (i)   the Defendant's costs of the claim summarily assessed in the sum of £1,500; less

    (ii)   a set off against such sum the damages award of £5.

3.   There be payment out forthwith of the monies in court and any interest thereon to the Defendants' solicitors without further order.

Dated this 4th **day of December 2002.**

this is the Defendants costs of the claims summarily assessed in the sum of £1,500 less a set off against such sum the damages award of £5.
"All stand" Mr Field Q.C. shot out of the rear door before I could get a word in. I just sat there bewildered could not believe it .
I had won the case up against a top Barrister. I am awarded £5 and had to pay the cost of the Solicitors who lost of £1,495 this is not British Justice but Freemason justice legal robbery.

I wrote to the Home Secretary they passed it on to the Court Services which is responsible for administration of Crown and County Courts in England and Wales. They replied. We cannot intervene in such decisions, or in the manner the case was conducted it would undermine the principle That the judiciary is entirely independent of Government.
I then wrote to the Office for the Supervision of Solicitors. They investigated my complaint which on and off over took 2 years.
They took no action against anyone. April 2004 I complained to the Legal Services Ombudsman. They replied 30 September. In the circumstances, while I realize this might disappoint you I take the view that the Law Society's (OSS)response to your complaint about Ms McAteer/Burton Copeland was satisfactory And the decision to close their file was justified. I got no justice one has to join the Freemasons.
You won't believe this but things get better, honestly.
On the corner of Duke Street and Linaker Street an old friend of mine Les Fairclough had a Antigue shop I called in for a chat and he showed me a copy of the Northwest Evening Mail. `Look at the property Eddie there are some cheap bargains in Cumbria`
He passed me the paper I spotted a photo of a large block of 15 flats, it was a huge detached white painted building and it was Freehold I rang the estate agent and made an appointment to view for tomorrow afternoon. I got the train and arrived in Barrow-in Furness at 2 p.m. Then caught a taxi to Ramsden Sreet the flats belong to Barrow Council. It was used for families waiting for council houses. It was in very good condition. After the agent showed me around I offered him the full asking price of £ 100,000.
He said he would send me contract out right away.
I asked for 2 months completion to give me more time.
Back on the train I was trying to think were I was going to raise the money, maybe I could sell it before I had bought it. It must be worth over £200,000 maybe my luck is changing. Don`t forget to succeed you need P.M.A Positive Mental Attitude. O.P.M. Other Peoples Money. I had the P.M.A. As a last resort I could find a partner but whom can you trust. It was no good trying the normal banks or building society's because you have to disclose any covictions for fraud if you fail to inform them you can be prosecuted.
The only way I could think of was a Non Status Bridging Loan I contacted Alisdair Devine Business &Investment Finance in Glasgow. He said that he could arrange a bridging loan of 65% of the valuation. On a valuation of £200,000 that would give me a loan of £130,000.But would I get a

valuation that high? There was only one way to find out. I instructed
BBG surveyors from Chester to do the valuation. Barrow Council lent me
the main door key to show the surveyor around. I did not want the
estate agent to come in case he mentioned the asking price. The
surveyor came and said he would walk around by himself.

"All the flats are open 15 in total" Off he went, years ago it was a hotel
called The Sun Hotel It must have 70 to 80 rooms on 3 floors. He came
back about 2 hours later.

"It's a huge building I have never seen so many rooms, I will have to
measure up now it will take me some hours."

"I can lend you a copy of the plans you can take measurements off
them" "That is great Mr O'Brien you have made my day. How much is
the asking price of the property?" "£200,000 it is freehold"

"Yes

"Which agent is selling the property?"

"No agent private sale with the vendor"

I could not disclose the agent because he would ring him for the sale
price. I had taken the for sale down sign down

A week later I received the valuation it was £160,000, that means I could
borrow £104,000 I was dancing. I sent the Valuation to Alisdair Divine
who passed it on to the bridging loan company. I was lucky because
most lenders will not allow you to select your own surveyor.

Before I returned the front door key to Barrow Council I had a copy
made so I could show potential buyers around without contacting the
selling agent. I had to sell it fast because I did not have the monthly
interest payments, in for a penny in for a pound. I asked a local estate
agent to come around as I might be putting it up for sale he would give
me an idea of the price to ask.

He gave me quite a shock."

"I would put it on at £300,000 then take an offer, do you want me to
advertise it?"

"Not yet I will let you now, thank you very much".

Better buy it first I was thinking. I received the offer letter from the
bridging bank they did not want accounts or income proof just as well

BARRON in FURNESS

I did not have any being on Income Support, the loan was purely on the property.

I advertised the property in Liverpool Echo, Manchester Evening News and the Asian times. If you want to sell a business put in the Asian Eye. With an income from the flats, 15 at £100 that's £1,500 per week,£78,000 per year it was a bargain at £300,000 I thought. There plenty off Asians interested as the Asian Times goes all over the U.K. A good place to advertise anything

The first viewer a Jewish property company from Manchester offered me £200,000

I just knew he wanted it   he went outside to make phone call   he came back in final offer £220,000

"NO "

He went out again came back £ 260,000

"NO"

I knew he wanted it but I was sweating'.

"The was the final offer I have other properties to see good day"

" I have lots of Asians coming later today I am certain they will top your offer .

You stupid   greedy bastard I felt sick greedy bastard .

He came back 20 minutes later " this is my final off £285,000. "

"Agreed"

It was completed 2 months later, my prayers were answered. Happy Days all I want now is a nice AFFECTIONATE lady to spoil but there will be no rush.

THE END

Eddie O'Brien. Born 1940, Butcher by trade, family man started with £1,000. Bought and sold 158 properties over 50 years and due to family treachery ended up on benefits. On benefits he borrowed £104,000 from a bank and made a killing making £185,000 in 8 weeks

You can do it. The secret of money dealing is O.P.M.

OTHER PEOPLES MONEY. A QUITTER NEVER WINS and a WINNER never QUITS.

Printed in Great Britain
by Amazon

83816616R00108